From Backwater to Mainstream

From Backwater to Mainstream

A PROFILE OF CATHOLIC HIGHER EDUCATION

by *Andrew M. Greeley*

with a commentary by *David Riesman*

First of a Series of Profiles Sponsored by
The Carnegie Commission on Higher Education

MC GRAW-HILL BOOK COMPANY
New York   St. Louis   San Francisco   London
Sydney   Toronto   Mexico   Panama

A number of colleagues at the National Opinion Research Center have worked with me in various stages of my research on Catholic Higher Education, and I am grateful for their help: Peter Rossi, James Davis, Norman Bradburn, William Van Cleve, Grace Ann Barry, Joe Spaeth. Nella Seifert handled the typing with her usual persistent carefulness. Nancy Morrisson was equally careful at the data-processing end of things. I wish also to thank the administrators, faculty, and students of Catholic colleges and universities who consented to what must have seemed on occasion as endless interviews. Among all such interviewees I want to single out for special mention Michael Walsh, the president of Fordham. I wish also to thank Howard Bobren at the Carnegie Commission on Higher Education for assembling much of the statistical data included in the Profile. I am also very grateful to the authors of the Foreword and the Commentary. To be sandwiched between Clark Kerr and David Riesman is a rare privilege.

Andrew M. Greeley

*The Carnegie Commission on Higher Education,
1947 Center Street, Berkeley, California 94704,
has sponsored preparation of this Profile as a
part of a continuing effort to present significant
information and issues for public discussion.
The views expressed are those of the author.*

FROM BACKWATER TO MAINSTREAM
A Profile of Catholic Higher Education

Foreword

Diversity is a hallmark of American higher education. It is seen not only in variations of size, organization, control, and appearance of colleges and universities, but also in such fundamental differences as their functions and their approaches to teaching and learning. As confusing as these differences sometimes may be, we value and encourage them because they enable our colleges and universities to serve an amazingly broad spectrum of individuals and groups within our highly pluralistic society.

As a contribution to a better understanding of the diversity in American institutions of higher learning, the Carnegie Commission on Higher Education intends to issue several reports that will contain comparable statistical and descriptive portraits of various types of institutions and their endeavors. This report on Catholic higher education is the first of these Profiles to be published.

Catholic colleges and universities share most of the goals and many of the problems of secular and Protestant institutions. Even so, they are distinctive in ways that such features as their names, their architecture and decor, or their faculty members' attire do not fully explain. They are warm and friendly, not only because they usually are small, but also because of the interest that faculty members, particularly some of the younger religious members, take in the students. They also tend to offer a general curriculum that gives strong emphasis to humanistic and philosophical disciplines. Perhaps it is because of these distinctions that graduates of Catholic colleges, despite tremendous changes in the Church itself, remain more satisfied with the education they have received and more loyal to their colleges than do alumni of other institutions.

Among the most recent and perceptive contributors to the serious study of Catholic higher education is Andrew M. Greeley, a young Catholic priest whose professional academic career, including graduate study, has been pursued at the University of Chicago. He is currently there as a program director in the National Opinion Research Center and is also professor of the sociology of education at the University of Illinois (Chicago). His perspective is unique, combining as it does his familiarity with Catholic institutions as a member of the clergy and the detachment that is part of his discipline as a social scientist. His earlier writings on this subject include *The Education of Catholic Americans* (1966) with Peter Rossi and *The Changing Catholic College* (1967) with William Van Cleve and Grace Ann Carroll.

Clark Kerr

Chairman
The Carnegie Commission
on Higher Education

September, 1969

Contents

1. Introduction and Historical Background

By now it is no longer a secret that Roman Catholicism is not the massive, smoothly organized, and efficiently operating monolith that many of its critics and defenders would like to have thought it was. Whatever remnants of the monolith myth may remain in one's mind are quickly put to rest when he begins to investigate the 350 colleges and universities which are affiliated with the Roman Catholic Church in the United States.[1]

The largest of the Catholic schools, Loyola University, in Chicago, has 12,631 students, a full-time staff of 546 (of whom 426 are laymen), and a part-time staff of 855 (of whom 840 are laymen). Sixty-four percent of the faculty have doctorates; the library has 462,000 volumes. Almost $10 million of federal funds went to Loyola in 1966. Eleven hundred thirty-five bachelors, 425 masters, 32 doctorates, and 212 professional degrees were awarded.

On the other hand, the College of Our Savior, at Amarillo, Texas, has two full-time students, six part-time students, and seven students in the summer session; two priests and six sisters with three masters and two bachelors constitute the faculty.

Somewhere in between is St. Mary's College, Orchard Lake, Michigan, with an enrollment of 131, of whom 45 are freshmen. The college's avowed purpose is to "provide priests and Catholic lay leaders to serve the people of Polish ancestry in the United States and Canada." The staff includes 25 people, and in 1966 ten bachelor's degrees were conferred.

The 350 schools may be called a "system" in some broad sense of the word because they are affiliated with the American Catholic Church, presumably receive information in the mail from the small staff of the college section of the National Catholic Educational

[1] The 350 schools are those listed in the 1967 edition of the *Official Guide to Catholic Educational Institutions*, excluding seminaries.

Association,[2] and have their names published in the *Catholic Educational Directory*. But beyond these rather tenuous bonds, there is neither organizational nor ideological unity within Catholic higher education, and the outside observer who expects that he will be able to generalize about this helter-skelter aggregation of schools soon realizes that he is skating on very thin ice. Everett Hughes once remarked that everything, sociologically speaking, had happened in and to the Roman Church. One might add that almost everything, educationally speaking, can be found in American Catholic higher education.

Immaculate Heart College, sitting on a smog-shrouded hill in Hollywood, is easily one of the most innovative and imaginative colleges in America.[3] Other schools seem barely to have emerged from the Middle Ages in their attitude toward education and toward students.[4] St. John's University in Minnesota, rooted in the German Benedictine tradition, presided over by an Irish president, has been a source of social and religious liberalism. One of the leading presidential candidates in 1968 was a graduate and a sometime faculty member of the school, as was a key man on the administrative staff of another presidential candidate.[5] On the other hand, the University of Dallas is a stronghold of staunch, right-wing conservatism, and some of its faculty members contribute frequently to right-wing journals.

Some institutions, most notably the University of Notre Dame, excel in the fine art of fund raising, while other institutions do not yet have, or even know about, consolidated budgets. The Catholic University of America has an outstanding department of Semitic languages, while other major Catholic universities have theology departments so painfully bad that even the student newspapers are reluctant to criticize them. Fordham boasted Marshall McLuhan and Margaret Mead on its staff. Other schools are lucky to have more than a handful of M.A.'s on their senior faculty. Student and faculty freedom at some institutions compares favorably with most American higher education, while other institutions still impose compulsory religious exercises on the students, routinely forbid

[2] Three people.

[3] It is currently locked in battle with the Cardinal Archbishop of Los Angeles.

[4] This comparison might be unfavorable to the Middle Ages.

[5] St. John's has other claims to fame, too, not the least of which is that pro football immortal Johnny "Blood" McNally was one of its graduates.

lectures by controversial speakers, and harass faculty members who get their names in the newspapers for saying things that outrage local conservatives.

The outstanding leaders in Catholic higher education at schools like Boston College, Holy Cross, Notre Dame, Fordham, St. Louis University, Webster College, St. John's of Minnesota, and Immaculate Heart of Los Angeles can hold their own with the very highest level of the educational establishment; and some of them, if it were not for their clerical status, would be candidates for cabinet positions in the national government. Some of the other college presidents never leave the campus of their schools, and it's probably just as well.

There are faculty members who are making $30,000 a year (though not very many), and others (though, again, not very many) who are making less than $5,000 a year. There are a few faculty members who teach hardly at all, and some who still teach 18 hours a week. Some schools have barely heard that there was a Second Vatican Council, and others are preparing for the day when they can have major influence at Vatican III. Some are seeking academic excellence with so great a hunger that they can almost taste it, and others are quite content to produce docile, upper-middle-class parishioners. Some are bent on being as secular as possible, while others are terrified that hiring even one non-Catholic faculty member may threaten their right to be called a Catholic college. Some of their faculty (and particularly the non-Catholic faculty) are enthusiastic and loyal to their schools, while others are openly critical and contend that the idea of a Catholic college is a contradiction in terms. Some schools live in mortal terror of their local bishop and others keep the bishop in mortal terror of them. Some cooperate closely with the bishop, and others pretend, more or less successfully, that he does not exist. Almost all the schools are in financial difficulty, but some face the future with hope and optimism and others with the grim conviction that their days are numbered, and they may well be.

It is, of course, possible to make some generalizations about Catholic higher education, and in this Profile we shall do so. The reader who is not familiar with the "system" ought to be warned beforehand that for every generalization we will make, there will be numerous exceptions. He should also realize that, because of the present considerable ferment within American Catholicism, he should be politely reserved about the generalizations made on Catholic higher education in the public press, whether they are made by the defenders or the critics of the "system."

Some general similarities among most of the schools may be noted: The presidencies of most of the schools are still held either by priests or by nuns.[6] The schools are subsidized, in some fashion or another, by the Church—either through the contributed services of the religious, or through direct financial support from a religious community or a diocese. They all represent some kind of commitment to the Roman Catholic faith, though the nature of this commitment varies from school to school, both in theory and in practice. Almost without exception, they were founded to serve the Catholic immigrant population and are now going, willy-nilly, through the process of adjusting to the needs of the Catholic population that is emerging from the immigrant experience. None of them is of the highest quality, as American academic standards go, though most would claim that they aspire to some kind of excellence which is simultaneously Catholic and American. Almost all of them are going through a period of questioning and self-doubt, and most have serious financial problems. Many, and probably most of them, feel quite inferior, at least at the subconscious level, to their non-Catholic competition.

TRENDS IN THE HISTORY OF CATHOLIC HIGHER EDUCATION

Approximately three-quarters of the Catholic schools have been founded in the present century (as Table 1 indicates), and more than 100 of them since 1950.[7] The largest institutions, however, those with over 5,000 students, with one exception, date to the last century. Most of the schools which have proliferated since 1950 are either junior colleges or the so-called sister formation colleges.

Those 350 schools that have survived into the present are but a minority of those which were founded, as Table 2 demonstrates.

---

[6] The new president of The Catholic University of America is a layman.

[7] Many of these 100 schools were sister formation schools founded to provide higher education for religious women, most of whom would be from Catholic grammar or high schools. But during the 1950s it was argued that such training should take place in special institutions which would then be affiliated with existing colleges or universities in some instances. More recently, however, nuns—as well as seminarians—have been educated in the same classrooms as lay students. It is unlikely that any more sister formation schools will be started, and many of them may be phased out.

Sixty-eight percent of the Catholic colleges for men founded prior to 1956 are no longer in existence. The time of highest casualties was the early 1900s from which only 4 of 35 schools survived to the present, and 24 were finished by 1920. But the survival rate in every decade of founding has been less than 50 percent until 1940, at which point the founding of colleges for men seems to have tapered off.

Most American higher educational institutions founded in the nineteenth century had a hard time staying alive, and Catholic institutions were no exception. The large amount of both founding and failure, however, seems surprising for an immigrant population that probably was not capable of sustaining very many colleges.[8] The explanation for this phenomenon is to be found in the relative independence of the Catholic religious orders and the reluctance of these independent bodies to cooperate with one another. Each religious community felt that it needed a college for training its own personnel and also laity who might be most sympathetic to it. Similarly, many of the nineteenth-century Catholic bishops felt that it was essential that they have a college to serve their own diocese, and as a result, the already thin resources which American Catholicism could devote to higher education were spread even thinner.

In his extremely important essay on the history of Catholic higher education, Philip Gleason (1967) comments:

It is hardly an exaggeration to say that Catholic higher education is entering its identity crisis in a state of virtual amnesia, with no meaningful grip on the history that has played so crucial a role in forging its present identity. It is supremely ironic that the Catholic academic community which is more and more disposed to accept the developmental review of reality, has only the sketchiest notion of the pattern of its own development. What is even more unfortunate and, from the developmental viewpoint simply bewildering, is the disposition sometimes manifested to treat the earlier efforts of Catholic educators with condescension or scorn because they are not what we are doing or trying to do today.

---

[8] Many institutions were founded in places where there was no significant Catholic population and were immediately foredoomed. Others, however, such as the University of Notre Dame, managed to survive their wilderness locale, although at least one high-level Notre Dame administrator was once heard to remark that he regretted that Father Sorin hadn't settled just a bit closer to Chicago. On the other hand, St. Mary of the Lake University, a diocesan college, was unable to survive even though it was in the heart of Chicago. It reappeared later as a seminary.

It would be no exaggeration, in fact, to say that American Catholicism almost lacks a history of its own and that the history of Catholic higher education is in even worse condition. There are a handful of first-rate scholars specializing in serious research on the historical development of American Catholicism, but given the magnitude and the complexity of the field, their work has only begun to furnish us with an understanding of the meaning of the American Catholic phenomenon. In the area of Catholic higher education there exists one comprehensive book written by Edward J. Power (1958). Only the history of The Catholic University of America, done by Ellis and his students (Ahern, Barry, and Hogan), the history of St. John's Abbey and University by Colman Barry (1956), and a few other works provide high-quality historical background for individual institutions. The Power book, while extremely

TABLE 1
Catholic higher educational institutions by period of founding

Catholic institu- tions	Period of founding							
	1786- 1799	*1800- 1824*	*1825- 1849*	*1850- 1874*	*1875- 1899*	*1900- 1909*	*1910- 1919*	*192*
Junior colleges (religious)							1	2
Junior colleges (lay)		1			3	1	1	3
Colleges (religious)	1				1		1	5
Colleges (under 1,000)		3	2	4	15	4	9	18
Colleges (1,000- 5,000)			10	15	17	9	11	16
Colleges (over 5,000)	1	1	4	10	4			
TOTAL	2	5	16	29	40	14	23	44

SOURCE: The Department of Education, United States Catholic Conference and Secretariat of the National Conference of Catholic Bishops, *The 1967 Official Guide to Catholic Educational Institutions and Religious Communities in the United States* (Catholic Institutional Directory Co., N.Y., 1967), hereinafter referred to as *The 1967 Official Guide to Catholic Educational Institutions.*

useful, has relatively little to say about the progress of Catholic higher education in the last 40 years, a time that would be of particular interest to those concerned with the changes of the past 5 or 10 years. But if Gleason is right when he says "the whole story of [Catholic higher education] may be understood in terms of the social evolution of the Catholic population and the institutional and ideological adjustments the colleges have made in order to adapt to the American scene without compromising their Catholicity," then we are hindered not only by lack of a social history of Catholic higher education, but also by lack of a comprehensive social history of the American Catholic population. Under such circumstances, the bewildered sociologist trying to deal with the contemporary phenomenon of Catholic higher education is forced to rely on impressions, guesses, and sweeping generalizations which, there is

)-	1940-1949	1950-1959	1960-1967	Total
	7	28	6	46
	4	11	9	35
	7	13	4	38
	9	17	7	108
	13	3	1	102
	1			21
	41	72	27	350

every reason to believe, the careful historians of the future will find somewhat more than just faintly amusing.

Nonetheless, we would think that some understanding of the historical development of Catholic higher education can be had if these three statements are kept in mind:

1 At the present time American Catholics are as likely to graduate from college as are other Americans.

2 Half the adult Catholics are either immigrants or the children of immigrants.

3 In Gleason's words, "the development of Catholic higher education has in fact followed the same general pattern as that of non-Catholic colleges and universities, but with a chronological lag."

The Catholic population is an immigrant population only now entering the mainstream of the social and economic life of the coun-

TABLE 2
Catholic colleges for men founded prior to 1956 and no longer in existence by period of founding and failure

Period of failure	Period of founding					
	1786-1799	1800-1824	1825-1849	1850-1874	1875-1899	1900-1909
1810-1819		1				
1820-1829		2				
1830-1839			1			
1840-1849		1	3			
1850-1859	1		7	5		
1860-1869		1	5	15		
1870-1879		1	1	15	1	
1880-1889				8	6	
1890-1899		1		5	7	
1900-1909			3	2	10	2
1910-1919				5	9	22
1920-1929			1	7	5	5
1930-1939				1	1	3
1940-1949					1	1
1950-1959						1
TOTAL	1	7	22	63	42	31
Still in existence	1	2	9	24	23	4
TOTAL	2	9	31	87	65	35
Percent failure	50%	78%	71%	72%	65%	88%

SOURCE: E.J. Power, *A History of Catholic Higher Education in the United States* (Bruce, Milwaukee, 1958).

try and, hence, its colleges and universities only now are turning aside from the posture of an immigrant religious group and taking on the posture of a typically American educational institution. It would be a mistake, however, to argue that there is some sort of historical inevitability in the process, that simply the passage of time and the development of an adequate social and economic base will lead to a system of Catholic higher education in which the range of schools from top to bottom will be not unlike the range of American higher education. It could very well be that there are some structural or ideological inhibitions built into the American Catholic social system which will prevent the social forces making for evolution of Catholic higher education from carrying the Catholic colleges along the path other schools have blazed but with ever-decreasing chronological lag.

A Look at Origins It is reasonably well known that the first Catholic college founded in this country was Georgetown in Washington, D.C., in the

1920- 1929	1930- 1939	1940- 1949	1950- 1956	Total
				1
				2
				1
				4
				13
				21
				18
				14
				13
				17
				37
1				22
2				8
	4			7
		2	1	4
3	4	2	1	182
0	3	9	5	85
3	7	11	6	267
100%	57%	18%	17%	68%

year 1789. After Georgetown, 82 more colleges were founded before the beginning of the Civil War. Of these, only 28 survive. In the decade before the Civil War, 41 colleges were formed, of which only 14 survive. (This fantastic rate of college foundation has continued unabated. Between 1904 and 1910, for example, 24 colleges were formed, of which none survive. At least for some of the years of the past decade it has been estimated that three Catholic colleges were founded each year, though in our present more enlightened age with financial help available from the Great Society program as well as the increased demand for college admission, the mortality rate among colleges is not nearly what it used to be.) For the most part, it would seem that these colleges were founded by missionary bishops in the American dioceses that were multiplying even more rapidly than were the institutions of higher education. The bishop, perhaps for reasons not altogether clear to himself, felt that it was one of his prime responsibilities in organizing a new diocese to establish a higher educational institution, a tradition that dates back to Archbishop Carroll's founding of Georgetown. However, only in rare instances was the bishop able to staff the college himself, and so one of the various religious orders was asked to take over first the staffing, and eventually the administration, of the school. Since the Jesuits were the most famous of Catholic educators, they were the ones a bishop most frequently would seek for his college. Some of the foundations were at best tenuous, and others which did manage to survive did so in many instances by the sheerest chance, especially since a good number of bishops, once they had called in a religious order to staff the college, left its success or failure, both financial and academic, entirely in the hands of the religious community.

It is fashionable to say that the colleges were founded to provide a place for the training of clerics, and surely it is true that much of what they did was in effect preseminary training, though the institutions were also founded to preserve the faith of those few Catholic lay people who sought a higher education. But it would be a mistake to feel that these two rather simple motivations were the only factors at work. It is to be suspected that a good number of bishops and college administrators in the early days of American Catholicism felt instinctively that an institution of higher education was something that was needed. If we casually read some of the letters of early American bishops, we can see that the idea of having a college of their own was something that was very dear to the hearts of most of them, and a respect for learning as an element in Catholic life appealed to the missionary bishops.

The schools were, for the most part, colleges in the European rather than in the English or contemporary American sense. They combined what we would now consider to be high school and college in one institution, joining three years of "academic" course work roughly equivalent to preparatory school and three years of "humanities" roughly equivalent to what we would consider college. However, given the poor state of primary education of the Catholic population, most of the early colleges were much more high schools than colleges in our sense. The curriculum was traditional, stressing the classics, rhetoric, and philosophy. Since the training received at these early Catholic colleges was a somewhat edited version of the famous Jesuit *ratio studiorum,* the philosophy of education, insofar as there was one behind such schools, tended to be static and conservative. It was assumed that the Catholic Church had an organic "integrity of vision" about the meaning of the world and of life, and it was the purpose of the college to pass on this vision of meaning to the student so he might have an integrated personality in an organic world view. The goal of Catholic higher education was then considered to be "the development of the whole man" (a cliché repeated consistently in Catholic college catalogs even today). The schools were not so much concerned with the pushing back of the frontier of truth as with passing on a given tradition of truth in which little in the way of addition or alteration was necessary.

It would be a mistake to assume that this static philosophy of education ended with the nineteenth century, or even that it is totally absent today. In Gleason's (1967) words:

To an age whose education was secular, scientific, and technical in spirit, particularized in vision, flexible in approach, vocational in aim, and democratic in social orientation, the Jesuits thus opposed a system that was religious, literary, and humanistic in spirit, synthetic in vision, rigid in approach, liberal in aim, and elitist in social orientation. There was no place in it for interchangeable parts, electivism, or vocationalism. These were simply the educational heresies that sprang from the radical defect, the loss of a unified view of reality. To tell a student that he could "elect" anything was to admit that one was no longer sure what was worth knowing, or the order in which it should be learned; to award a degree to those who elected this, that, and the other thing until the whole collection added up to 128 "credits" was utter academic and intellectual irresponsibility.

In a famous address to "the assembled Faculties of the largest Catholic University in the world," Father Bull[9] argued that Catholicism was a culture, a way of life, a view of reality; that the characteristic mark of this view of reality was its totality of vision, the way it ordered all knowledge and values into a comprehensive organic unity; and that it was the function of the Catholic college to impart to students this Catholic culture, this synthetic vision.

A few years later, Father Bull argued in another essay that the function of the Catholic graduate school was precisely the same as that of the Catholic college, only on a higher level; he specifically denied that research was the function of the graduate school. In fact, he asserted, to accept the primacy of research would be to attempt "the impossible task of being Catholic in creed and anti-Catholic in culture." Research as an *"attitude,"* Bull declared, was concerned not with truth, but with the *"pursuit of truth";* its tendency was vocational and particularistic, "its spontaneous bent [was] toward the apotheosis of the principle of disintegration," and its ultimate consequence was dehumanization. Between the Catholic view and the research view there were only antinomies—organic unity vs. disintegration; the "sense of tradition and wisdom achieved vs. 'progress'; . . . principles vs. fact; . . . contemplation vs. 'research.'" Education at the graduate level, as elsewhere, was for Bull, "the enrichment of human personality, by deeper and deeper penetration into the velvety manifold of reality, as *Catholics possess it."*

This view of the purpose of higher education is certainly held by relatively few Catholic educators today (though it is not by any means absent from their official statements of purpose) nor was it a universal position even 30 to 40 years ago, but it represents a deeply felt system of goals that profoundly influenced Catholic higher education in its formative years and remains, at least in its residual effects, part of the Catholic higher educational picture.

The typical college administrator (unless he served one of the few lay-founded colleges that did not last very long) was a member of a religious order, and his qualifications as a president or a dean were primarily his seminary training. The faculty members were chosen from the religious community, though even at the beginning there were a few lay auxiliaries, men whose role as second-class citizens was all too clear. The students were not entirely future seminarians, though this made little or no difference in their life, since the rigidly structured and closely supervised academic

---

[9] Father Bull was a professor of philosophy at Fordham University, which was the school that he accurately described at that time as the largest Catholic university in the world.

life of the future layman was precious little different from that of the future cleric.

Thus, at the beginning of the twentieth century Catholic colleges were small, in constant financial difficulty, academically inferior, static in educational philosophy, traditional in curriculum and pedagogy, rigid in discipline and student life, clerical in faculty administration, and isolated almost completely from the mainstream of American higher education. On the other hand, it is worth noting that many of the faults then, as now, were also found in most other American colleges and universities.

Into the Twentieth Century Between 1900 and the end of World War II four major developments contributed to the forward academic movement of Catholic colleges as well as their movement toward a closer relationship with other American colleges. (1) Under pressure of the college division of the Catholic Educational Association, the six-year college curriculum was revised into a four-year preparatory school curriculum and a four-year college program with gradual divorce of the preparatory school from the college—a divorce which was not completed in many of the Jesuit institutions until the early 1920s. (2) At the same time pressures from the CEA and from powerful theorists within the Catholic colleges forced the schools to move toward a greater standardization of program and curriculum requirements with the gradual adoption of the credit system. (3) Such a process was accelerated by the increasing need to meet the requirements of the accrediting agencies, although many Catholic schools were reluctant to adopt the "secularist" standards of these agencies, which were felt by Catholic accrediting agencies of the old school to be at variance with the integrated and organic nature of Catholic education. For example, St. John's University in Minnesota moved toward accreditation only in the years after World War II. (4) In the midst of the process of accreditation, standardization, and curriculum reform, many of the Catholic schools also became universities, not so much by moving into doctoral programs (only The Catholic University of America was truly a doctoral school), but rather by acquiring various professional schools, such as engineering, law, commerce, medicine, music, and journalism. The favorite way of converting a college into a university was not so much to found a new school as to purchase or pick up by default one of the many small and faltering professional schools that could be found in the major metropolitan areas—

a method popular with non-Catholic urban schools as well.[10] This "instant transformation" from a small liberal arts college into a multipurpose university was justified on the very persuasive grounds that the school's role in a large city was to serve the many needs of the urban population. Such schools also provided professional training for many Catholics in the metropolis who otherwise might not have obtained it or might have obtained it under what would be deemed dangerous, non-Catholic auspices. Whether one thinks this transformation into an "instant university" was greatly courageous or foolhardy depends upon his point of view. In any event, the move was made and, with the exception of the medical schools, it does not seem to have been financially unprofitable. Whether the concentration on professional schools inhibited the development of a more academic atmosphere in the Catholic colleges remains to be seen, although we are readily persuaded that at least the Catholic medical schools represent a tremendous drain on the resources, time, and personnel of Catholic universities.

What would have happened in the development of Catholic education in the years after World War I if the catastrophe of the Great Depression had not struck the United States is unclear. However, between 1928 and 1940 the only possible role that occurred to most Catholic administrators was survival. It should be kept in mind that many of the men in the senior administrative positions in the Catholic universities at the present time, and the major superiors of the orders that oversee the universities, went through their formative years during the Great Depression and have yet to be persuaded in their heart of hearts that it could not happen again.

The Postwar Decades   To the many college administrators who had managed to survive World War II only with the help of various officer-training programs, the years immediately after were an incredible experience, half dream and half nightmare. Where previously there had been not enough students and too many faculty, there was now an overwhelming number of students and not nearly enough faculty.

[10] For the fascinating story of how Marquette University managed to collect virtually every professional school in Milwaukee that was not "nailed down," see Hamilton (1953). The book is also interesting for its accounts of the almost incredible financial problems and manipulations of Marquette in its early days, as well as for its rather bold introduction of the principle of coeducation.

While some argued that the schools should limit their enrollment and continue to be what they were—small liberal arts colleges— this counsel to prudence was ignored, and the Catholic colleges expanded at a fantastic rate in the late 1940s. The expansion jolted to a temporary stop during the Korean conflict (a stop that acutely embarrassed some of the smaller schools that had over-expanded) and then proceeded at even more frantic rates of growth until the present time. Thus, in 1916 there were 32,000 students enrolled in Catholic colleges, many of them in the precollege pre-paratory programs. By 1930 there were 102,000, and by 1940 the numbers had inched up to 162,000. At the present time, the enrollment is around 400,000, more than twice what it was a quarter of a century ago, and more than 140,000 above the enroll-ment in 1960. Not only did the enrollments in the schools them-selves go up, but the number of schools expanded as well, so that at the present time there are over 300 Catholic institutions of higher education, the exact number depending on how many of the seminaries and the small sister formation colleges one wishes to count as institutions of higher learning. This expan-sion has largely been uncontrolled because, despite the impres-sion that many non-Catholics have, American Catholicism is a loosely organized institution with little in the way of centralized control and direction. Any bishop can permit the foundation of a college within his diocese, and any religious superior can, either at the invitation of the bishop or on his own initiative, propose that a new college be formed. In the Chicago standard statistical metropolitan area alone, for example, there are, if one counts the seminaries and sister formation schools, more than 25 Catholic schools claiming to offer higher education. In addition, despite a good deal of happy talk, any institutional collaboration that does exist besides the theoretical is very minimal indeed.[11]

Along with this pell-mell expansion there has been a tendency toward laicization and professionalization on the Catholic cam-puses out of sheer necessity. Laymen in large numbers had to be hired to serve the needs of the post-World War II students who

[11] Many of the other religious orders are extremely critical of the Jesuits for their refusal to engage in interinstitutional cooperation. They contend that the Jesuits presiding over 28 institutions of higher learning and playing a controlling role in American Catholic higher education are academic imperialists who simply do not even want to recognize the existence of other colleges. While such charges would be demonstrably false if leveled against certain Jesuit administrators, there seems little reason to doubt that it is true in a fair number of instances.

inundated the Catholic campuses. It gradually and painfully became clear that the old familial patterns of relationships that
existed among faculties when most members were clerics were no
longer appropriate. Even though the change has been slow and
not nearly as enthusiastic as the lay faculty members or the liberal Catholic critics would like, the gradual replacement of familial norms with professional norms is continuing and accelerates
with each passing year.

Furthermore, Catholic universities since the end of World
War II have moved toward the establishment of authentic arts
and sciences graduate schools. While only The Catholic University of America can claim admission in the strict sense to the fra-
ternity of true universities (granting 1 percent of the Ph.D.'s in the
country), there are several other Catholic institutions that are
seriously planning to become major graduate institutions, and
still others that are flirting with the idea without counting the
costs or the problems. In our judgment, at the present time there
are at least four, and possibly five, metropolitan areas where
major Catholic graduate centers would be technically, academically, and economically feasible.[12] Gleason's comments are once
again singularly appropriate: "No one would deny that there is
still room for much more improvement, but it is equally important to recognize, in evaluating the present situation, that graduate work on the doctoral level is hardly older than yesterday in
Catholic universities."

Finally, in the years since the end of the war, there has been
a considerable amount of talk, and not an inconsiderable amount
of activity, directed toward the entry of Catholic academia into
the mainstream of American higher education. John Tracy Ellis'
famous essay in 1955 about the failures of Catholic intellectualism in this country both symbolized and accelerated the pace of
this development. The "quest for excellence" in the Catholic colleges, while in many instances misdirected and in other instances
abortive, is nonetheless sincere (at least more or less so) and
powerful. Gleason notes that:

Adjustment was an ongoing process of accommodation, responding to
this pressure or that need as it became noticeable to the point of demand-
ing action. Catholic educators have always been struggling to keep up
with the situation; they have never been able to get on top of their prob-

---

[12] Chicago, New York, Boston, and San Francisco could certainly support major
Catholic universities. Some will contend that so can Washington and St. Louis.

lems or to dispose matters according to some ideal scheme. The same is largely true of all American educators, of course, but there are some special complexities involved with Catholic institutions. All colleges and universities had to adjust themselves to changing needs in American society, but Catholic educators had the additional problem of adapting their adjustments to the general pattern followed by non-Catholic institutions.[13]

But the transition in which American Catholicism presently finds itself as the universal Church moves from the counterreformation to the ecumenical age and its American branch from the immigrant slum to the upper-middle-class suburb is not a smooth one, and the adaptations of which Gleason speaks are doubly difficult at the present time. Three developments in particular ought to be mentioned to conclude our brief historical sketch.

1   During 1966 there was a sudden and dramatic trend toward "secularization" of Catholic higher education. While the word meant many things to many people, it has been used to cover a series of phenomena in which the educational institutions obtained some degree of freedom from the religious orders which had previously owned them. Webster College, St. Louis, Missouri, began the movement when its president left the religious life but remained as head of the college and formal ownership was transferred from the Sisters of Loretto to a lay board of trustees. At the present time, numerous schools have some form of secularization, of which the most typical is a mixed board of trustees, partly religious and partly lay, with the proviso that the president of the college must be a member of a religious order. There were a number of reasons for this dramatic change. First of all, partial or total laicization of the board of trustees was in keeping with the theories of the Vatican Council on the layman's role in the Church. Secondly, such laicization of the trustees placed the Catholic colleges in a better legal position to receive federal aid. Thirdly, the independence of the colleges from the religious orders gave college administrations more freedom of movement and removed from the religious orders very heavy financial responsibility.

In "liberal" Catholic circles the laicization of the boards of trustees was greeted with considerable enthusiasm, and when some observers, such as the present writer and Prof. David Ries-

[13] This synopsis is based on my own summary in *The Changing Catholic College,* which in its turn relies heavily on Philip Gleason's paper.

man, suggested that the so-called laicization of control might not
accelerate educational progress and might, in fact, even hinder
it, the reaction from these liberals "was one of stunned disbelief
that anyone could be so misguided." However, as Professor
Riesman has observed, Catholic business and professional men
are less likely to be well informed about educational matters than
were the members of the religious community that preceded them
on the board of directors. Further, the trustees are, in most if not
all cases, chosen by the incumbent administration of the university, which will mean that at least for some time to come the
trustees will merely reinforce the position of the administration.
A progressive administration will have its hand strengthened;
a conservative one will be able to be free from the threat of being
ejected from office by a liberal, provincial, or general of the religious order.

2   At the same time, the financial problem which has always been
    serious in Catholic higher education became acute due, for the
    most part, to dramatic increases in faculty salaries. Whether
    the economic woes in the Catholic higher educational institutions
    are any worse, proportionally, than those of most private colleges
    would be hard to say, though the Catholic schools probably had
    less in the way of financial resources to start with and have been
    harder hit by the current crisis than many other private schools.
    If one can say, as a broad generalization, that American private
    higher education will not survive without considerable financial
    help from government and private industry, it could also be said
    that, in the absence of this help, the Catholic colleges may well
    be among the first to slip out of existence.

3   The constant debate within American Catholicism over whether
    there ought to be Catholic schools or Catholic colleges and uni-
    versities has reached a new fever pitch in the wake of the Vatican
    Council. Secularization of the boards of trustees, total or partial,
    and the extreme financial crisis have made the controversy more
    pertinent and more bitter. The tools of scholarship are rarely
    brought to bear to clarify the issues of this controversy, and when
    they are, they are frequently misused. While the majority of Amer-
    ican Catholics and the majority of American Catholic educators
    are probably still committed to a distinctive higher educational
    "system," the minority which wishes to eliminate the "system"[14]

---

[14] And apparently their own jobs, too.

is articulate, has ready access to influential Catholic journals, and is in firm possession of the dialectical initiative.

Thus, American Catholicism is in the final phases of its acculturation process as the Catholic population becomes thoroughly American. Catholic higher education, therefore, is also definitively departing from its original position within the walls of the immigrant ghetto, attempting to become part of the broader American higher educational enterprise. The final phases of such a shift would have been painful and difficult in any event, but the three complications described in the preceding paragraphs make the transition even more difficult. Hence, one is forced to be cautious in predicting how Catholic higher education will survive in the remaining decades of the present century. It is most unlikely that Catholic schools will simply cease to be. It is also most unlikely that they will continue to increase in numbers as they have done in the past. Given broad federal aid to Catholic higher education, many if not most of the Catholic colleges will probably survive, and some (though one hesitates to say many) will probably become quite indistinguishable in procedures and quality from some of the best of the second-level colleges and universities.

Another way of concluding this historical introduction is to say that the Catholic higher educational problems of the United States were initially far more Catholic than they were American, and through the years of acculturation have become more and more American problems and less and less specifically *Catholic* problems. It is a matter of debate among observers at the present time whether the current problems of the Catholic schools arise in great part from the fact that they are Catholic, or can be traced, rather, in great part to the fact that they are American. Most of those within the Catholic "system," whether they be defenders or critics of the Catholic colleges and universities, will argue vigorously that there are many uniquely and specifically Catholic problems. On the other hand, sympathetic observers from outside the "system" are frequently inclined to contend that while there may be some problems that are uniquely Catholic, most of the difficulties that Catholic higher educational institutions experience are difficulties they have in common with almost all private educational institutions of similar size and resources. The writer of this Profile is inclined to the latter position.

2. Atmosphere of Catholic Colleges

There is a subtle atmosphere which enables the sensitive observer to know rather quickly that he is on a Catholic college campus. The religious names of dormitory halls, the clerical garb of many of the teachers, religious symbols such as crucifixes and statues, the chapel (which is frequently the most impressive building on campus), the ease with which students seem to slip into churches or chapels for religious services, the title of "Father" or "Sister" or on rare occasions "Brother" addressed to certain faculty members, the frequently somewhat aloof reticence of those who possess these titles, the informality which many of the clerical administrators try to maintain with their colleagues—all these mark the Catholic campus as just a bit different to someone who visits for the first time.

It is difficult to separate religious from socioeconomic and ethnic variables. The young people on Catholic campuses look clean-cut and well groomed, though beards are beginning to appear. Only a few students are antagonistic toward faculty and administration, and admiration for teachers—particularly members of the religious order—is widespread, even though the religious no longer win respect ipso facto. Social action projects, usually of the "volunteer" variety, draw substantial numbers of recruits. Among the young women, particularly at the all-female colleges, there is a touch of serious intellectualism which is unsophisticated enough to be quite charming. But intellectual interest is not extremely high, though the students are apparently willing to work quite hard at their assignments.

There is also more warmth and friendliness—if not friendship—among the students and between students and faculties at Catholic colleges than one would find at most secular campuses. The friendliness may at times be pseudo-gemeinshaft in substance, but on some campuses it is real enough. Resentment seems more latent than at many other schools, and administrators and faculty tend to know more about the personalities and backgrounds of their students than they would in the secular school. Sometimes this greater friendliness and intimacy may have strong paternalistic tinges; but in its best manifestations it can be an extremely attractive dimension of campus life.

Perhaps the most important contribution to the different atmosphere of Catholic colleges is the dedication of the religious. One need not ignore the paternalism, emotional manipulation, exploitation, and frustration that frequently characterize the relationship between these celibates and their charges; but it still seems to the present observer that there is much that is healthy and positive in many relationships between the religious and the students. It is not at all improbable that the greater loyalty of Catholic alumni (to be reported in a later chapter), despite realistic appraisal of the weaknesses of their schools, is directly related to the many warm and satisfying relationships between students and members of the religious orders. One of the great weaknesses of Catholic higher education has been its failure to create a culture and a structure where the benefits of these relationships could be maximized.

The atmosphere of warmth, informality, friendliness—blended with more explicit religious terminology than is usually heard in modern society—may not be everyone's cup of tea, not even, in fact, every Catholic's cup of tea. It is very easy for it to become artificial, paternalistic, and unprofessional. But at its best, it represents a quality of humaneness of which American higher education could use more, rather than less.

But if Catholic institutions share some elements to be found in the atmosphere of their campuses, there are also vast diversities in mood and quality present. The most famous, and in some ways the best, of the universities is Notre Dame, sprawled across thousands of acres of northern Indiana countryside. Notre Dame is best known, of course, for its powerful football teams, which, if not quite the threat they used to be in the days of Coach Frank Leahy, are nonetheless a menace to all their foes. It is fashionable in intellectual circles, Catholic as well as non-Catholic, to deprecate Notre Dame's football team, but the fame and fortune that the team has brought to the school has made academic improvement possible. The Notre Dame faculty, quite conscious of how the football team helps to make up the annual budget, are not so ready to deprecate the accomplishments of the Fighting Irish. A substantial portion of the Notre Dame faculty—no one knows how high a proportion, because Notre Dame does not inquire as to its faculty members' religion—is non-Catholic. Its students are, for the most part, from upper-middle-class families, but unlike almost every other Catholic institution, Notre Dame is a national university whose enrollment is not limited to one geographic area. The campus includes such architectural contradictions as its famed Byzantine golden dome, a Gothic chapel, a giant library which has been uncharitably compared to a grain elevator,[1] and a geodesic dome student center.

Similarly, Notre Dame's academic development has been a strange mixture; it has traditionally been strong in chemistry and some of the physical sciences. Its psychology department, however, is of very recent vintage—largely because one of its former presidents who later became a cardinal had grave suspicions of anything that resembled psychology. But even though the rate of growth among the Notre Dame departments is not uniform, there has been, particularly in the last decade, a steady improvement in the overall quality of the university. In addition, under the imaginative leadership of its president, Father Theodore Hesburgh, and its elder statesman, Dr. George Shuster, Notre Dame has pioneered such innovations as the Center for the Study of Man in Contemporary Society and an Institute for Advanced Religious Studies. Furthermore, it has taken the lead among American Catholic universities in wrestling with problems of birth control, population, and abortion. Notre Dame impresses the visitor as a bustling Midwestern institution which is very much alive. If there be a Catholic multiversity, Notre Dame is the place.

But in the process of becoming a multiversity, Notre Dame may also have lost contact with its undergraduate students; the old religious forms no longer seem to appeal to the very bright young men who attend it. Some of Notre Dame's faculty feel that the increase in deviant religious forms, particularly of a Catholic Pentecostal group, is a sign that anomie is replacing the rigid gemeinschaft of an earlier Notre Dame.

Its closest rivals—Boston College, Fordham, and St. Louis—

---

[1] The south side of this giant library has a great mosaic of Jesus extending his hands in benediction to the world. Some of the more irreverent students have nicknamed this mosaic "touch-down Jesus," a joke which, once it has been heard, is a distraction to serious TD football viewing.

would probably be prepared to concede that Notre Dame is the pacesetter in publicity, if not in reality. The neutral observer from the outside would not want to be put in the position of making comparisons, but he would be forced also to say that as Notre Dame goes, so probably goes American Catholic higher education. If American Catholicism is able to produce a viable form of higher education for the new Catholic upper middle class, then Catholic higher education will survive. If it can be done, it will be done at Notre Dame; and if Notre Dame fails to do it, if for no other reasons than symbolic ones, it is a safe prediction that no one else will.

At the other end of the scale, not of quality, but of institutionalization, is Immaculate Heart College in Los Angeles. Set on a small smog-shrouded hill in a run-down section of Hollywood, Immaculate Heart, with substantially less than a thousand students, makes no claim to academic greatness. It has no desire to be a multiversity; in fact, it has no desire to be anything but itself—and many of those who have visited it would unhesitatingly say that no one could ask for anything more. Immaculate Heart College is, to its admirers (and the present writer is unashamedly one of them), one of the most unique human institutions in the world. It is a place where casual, unselfconscious laughter manifests the spirit of openness and trust which the visitor dimly perceives may be the goal of much human striving.

Immaculate Heart will shortly leave behind its dilapidated building in Hollywood to migrate to the Claremont campus; presumably it will bring with it its folk art museum, its freewheeling innovations, its serigraph art of Mary Corita Kent, the inspired madness of its "Mary's Day," and above all, the joy and laughter which make it seem like an oasis in a desert when one is touring American higher education institutions. If Immaculate Heart can survive its financial crisis and keep alive its unique spirit in the Claremont group, then anyone who visits it will not wonder whether there is a unique Catholic contribution in American higher education.

The two strongest Jesuit competitors in Catholic higher education are Boston College and Fordham, and at the present time the past of Boston College and the future of Fordham are very much involved with the personality of one of the great Jesuit college presidents— Reverend Michael Walsh. Until last year the president of Boston College, Walsh presided over what Prof. David Riesman has called "the miracle of Chestnut Hill." He became president of Fordham in the midst of the latter university's acute financial crisis. Father Walsh has been characterized (with admiration) by the present writer as "Spencer Tracy playing Frank Skeffington in *The Last Hurrah.*" Possessing all the charm, wit, and political skill which characterize the Boston Irish, Walsh also has extraordinarily acute academic sensitivities and shrewd financial instincts. The progress at Boston College under his leadership has been gradual and careful; at Fordham he will have to contend with a school that slumbered for many years and then suddenly made a huge leap forward, and in the process of the leap, acquired debts which call into question its very existence. Both Boston College and Fordham could be considered presentable third-level universities. In most sections of the country other than the Northeast, they would be looked to for community leadership and would be the object of great pride to both their students and faculty. But Boston College is not Harvard and never will be; and Fordham is not Columbia or NYU and never will be. Neither faculty nor students (and the latter are some of the most sophisticated in the country) are able to get over the fact that they are not as good as their neighbors. This feeling of inferiority is reinforced by a wider inferiority complex which, at least to a Middle Western Catholic, seems to be one of the grave weaknesses of East Coast Catholicism. Boston College and Fordham could both become presentable urban universities deeply concerned with the social problems of their respective metropolises, bringing to these metropolises a Catholic concern for the underprivileged and the suffering (some of whom may not be financially underprivileged at all). But it will take all the charisma that leaders like Mike Walsh are able to generate to overcome the feelings of inferiority that arise whenever a comparison is made with the great institutions across the river—whether the river be the Charles or the East.

Far from Chestnut Hill and the Bronx, on the prairies of Stearn County, Minnesota, one turns off the highway, drives down a short road, and encounters one of the most extraordinary buildings of the Western hemisphere—Marcel Breuer's St. John's Abbey Church. The monastery has been for many years the center of liturgical and social reform for American Catholicism, and its college, while never exploiting to the fullest the riches of the monastery tradition, is nevertheless an excellent example of how Benedictine monastic traditions can be translated into an American higher educational medium. A strong faculty receiving as high sal aries as any American Catholic institution, an enthusiastic alumni, a spirited student body, and imaginative leadership make St. John's one of the most attractive Catholic undergraduate institutions in the country. Whether the Benedictine tradition with its deep roots in the land and its strong, warm community ties can survive in the United States may yet be uncertain, but St. John's is a brave and vigorous attempt; the outsider can only wish that the Benedictines would be more forthright and explicit in their creative attempt to translate Benedictinism into Stearns County English.

St. John's and the other Benedictine schools represent a tradition of monastery education going back even before the birth of the European university. The women's colleges administered by the religious of the Sacred Heart are a modern manifestation of the French convent school for the daughters of well-to-do families. One who is familiar with the history of the religious of the Sacred Heart but has never encountered them directly would expect Newton, Barat, Manhattanville, and the other Sacred Heart schools to be stuffy, old-fashioned institutions which protect and isolate their well-to-do females from an ugly and dirty world. But even though there is much that is quaint in the Sacred Heart style (and only some of it has been removed by their recent reforms), preconceived stereotypes have to be put aside shortly after one walks onto their campuses. The customs and the language may be quaint, but the deep personal concern for the students which the religious manifest and the affection with which the girls respond are anything but quaint; nor is the intense academic interest[2] nor the deep social awareness which the Sacred Heart colleges produce in some of their alumnae. American Catholicism has thus far produced only a rather small aristocracy, but the aristocratic women who have graduated from the Sacred Heart schools (including many of the distaff members of the Kennedy clan) are sufficient evidence that even the egalitarian society (which isn't very egalitarian) can use some charming aristocrats.

As one adviser of the Sacred Heart religious pointed out to me, "They have something special there, but it's hard to say quite what it is." The religious of the Sacred Heart are busily engaged in ex-

[2] The present writer and his team of NORC researchers were somewhat bowled over when entering the lobby of Newton College of the Sacred Heart early on a winter morning to see a large bundle of *New York Times* at the entrance and some two score of students sitting around in funeral-parlor silence devouring the latest "official" version of the day's events.

panding their work to include the working class and the under-privileged, quite confident that whatever their "something special" is, it will not be lost if it spreads beyond the boundaries of the aristocracy.

In the midst of the dark canyons of the Chicago Loop, in one of the older skyscrapers of that ethnic city, is the downtown campus of De Paul University, administered by the same religious community which experienced near disaster at St. John's University in Long Island. De Paul is unabashedly a commuter university. Its downtown campus and crowded near Northside center are staging grounds for the offspring of ethnic immigrant groups on the journey from the "old neighborhood" to the "new suburb." De Paul makes no claim to be an academically elite school but takes great pride in the number of its law graduates who occupy key positions in the city, state, and national governments; in its usually successful basketball team; and in its availability to the children of the more recent arrivals in American society. There are no dormitories at De Paul, and only a handful of academic doctorate programs, but the elaborate and informal sorority system is an important decompression chamber for young women who are the first in their family to attempt higher education.[3] For many De Paul students attending college, much less a graduate school, this is a dramatic break with the past. Some would have made the break even if De Paul were not there, but the Catholicity of the school provides reassurance to many who, one suspects, would have found the leap from the Northwest side ethnic neighborhood to the state university too big to attempt.

As one enters the main quadrangle of Spring Hill College in Mobile, Alabama, and sees the long and somewhat dilapidated Southern veranda, he almost expects to see Burl Ives sitting in a rocking chair chewing tobacco and announcing to one and all that he was, indeed, "Big Daddy." Spring Hill is one of the oldest American Catholic colleges, but, being located far from the main centers of Catholic population, it has not grown rapidly. The faculty is not, by academic standards, distinguished. Its students are frequently young men and women whose academic qualifications were not such that they could get into other Catholic institutions, or who were attracted to Spring Hill by its weather, its golf course,

---

[3] One De Paul law student remarked, "If you can't be a sorority queen at least once during your four years at De Paul, you have to have something wrong with you."

and its claim to be the "country club of the South." But whatever may be said of the past of Spring Hill, its present leadership is not symbolized by the sleepy and faintly decadent appearance of its oldest buildings. Spring Hill has no illusions; the best it ever hopes to be is a "Catholic Emory," and it knows it has a long way to go. But it hasn't given up, is willing to experiment, and is quite legitimately proud that it was one of the first colleges in the South to have an integrated student body.

Notre Dame, Boston College, Fordham, Immaculate Heart, St. John's, De Paul, Spring Hill, and the Sacred Heart schools represent the vast diversity of atmospheres and goals that can be found in American Catholic higher education. After a year of touring such diverse institutions, the present writer and his colleagues concluded that only fiction could adequately convey the ferment, the hope, and the fears to be observed on these campuses, as Catholicism struggles through its twin transitions from slum to suburbs and from counterreformation to ecumenical age. At none of the schools mentioned in this chapter is the quality of education unbearably bad—as American standards go; neither, however, can any of the schools claim the prestige of any of the great state universities or the best of the liberal arts colleges. The response of the most honest Catholic administrators would be that the atmosphere made possible by the religious tradition and commitment compensates for the lower prestige of its faculty. The present writer would add that he is convinced that religious tradition and commitment can create an atmosphere in which the total personal growth of some young people will be more effectively facilitated than it would be in other institutions. Not all Catholic institutions, by any stretch of the imagination, do provide an atmosphere that makes much difference, but some do. The future of Catholic education in the United States probably depends on how many Catholic schools can combine scholastic excellence, if not eminence, with a distinctive atmosphere that facilitates the personal growth of the students.

3. Statistical Overview

If one excludes the seminaries from consideration, there are, as Tables 3 and 4 demonstrate, 52 all-male colleges which contain approximately one-fourth of the students in Catholic colleges, 223 women's colleges which also contain one-fourth of the students, and 75 coeducational institutions which contain one-half of the students. The 46 junior colleges for members of such communities are, with 5 exceptions, run by religious orders of women for the education of their own members. While they represent 24 percent of all the Catholic colleges, they have only 2 percent of the students and are included in this analysis precisely because data on them are essential if one is not to have a distorted view of the implications of the very large number of Catholic colleges.

Junior colleges for members of the religious orders are all quite small — the largest having a total enrollment of 139, of which 74 are part time. The largest exclusively full-time school has a total enrollment of 71. The four-year colleges for members of religious orders are also quite small; the largest has an enrollment of 861, the second largest has an enrollment of 738, and the third largest has an enrollment of 427. Half of the schools have a total enrollment under 100, and a little over one-third of the schools have a total enrollment under 50.

There is, further, a considerable difference in the distribution of students in the men's, women's, and coed schools. The men's schools tend to be somewhat larger, with 63 percent enrolling more than 1,000 students (accounting for 92 percent of the students in these institutions). On the other hand, 82 percent of the women's schools have an enrollment under 1,000 and contain within their classrooms 55 percent of the students in the women's colleges.

The 15 coeducational schools with over 5,000 enrollment represent only one-fifth of the coeducational colleges but enroll three-fifths of the coeducational students. Similarly, the 6 all-male schools with enrollment over 5,000 represent only 11 percent of the institutions but enroll 39 percent of the students. The 21 Catholic colleges with enrollments over 5,000 represent only 6 percent of all institutions but enroll 40 percent of the students who attend Catholic higher educational institutions, and about one-third of all Catholic students are to be found in the 15 coeducational institutions with enrollments over 5,000. Thus, one must be careful when one speaks of what is typical in Catholic higher education. If by "typical" one means the modal college, the typical Catholic school would be a women's college with enrollment under 1,000. But if by "typical" one means that institution in which a student is most likely to be found, then the typical institution is a coeducational college with enrollment of more than 5,000. Either method of analysis is valid, but one ought to specify very clearly whether he is speaking of institutions or students. One must also be aware of the kind of analysis which would attribute one "vote" to a sister formation college with less than 50 students and one "vote" to the University of Notre Dame with over 6,000.

Table 5 lists the 21 Catholic universities with enrollments of over 5,000. Only six of these schools—Loyola, Marquette, St. John's, St. Louis, Fordham, and Dayton—have enrollments of over 10,000 (all but St. John's and Dayton are Jesuit schools). Marquette, with 9,638 students, has the largest full-time enrollment, and Boston College, with 8,118, is second in full-time enrollment.

In Table 6 we turn to the distribution by sex of students in the Catholic higher educational institutions. One-half of all the males in Catholic colleges are in institutions with over 5,000 students, as are one-quarter of the females. Furthermore, the large colleges— that is to say, the ones with over 5,000 students—are about seven-tenths male. Then, if one can say that the men are most likely to be in the large schools and also that these schools will be heavily male in their composition, similarly women are more likely to be in the medium-sized schools (between 1,000 and 5,000 enrollment) and in institutions where the sex ratio is relatively equal.

Just as the Catholic population is concentrated in the Northeast and North Central sections of the country, so is Catholic higher education. Two hundred sixty-seven Catholic schools, or 76 percent, are found in the Northeast and North Central sections

Catholic higher educational institutions	Male		Female	
	Number	Percent	Number	Percen
Junior colleges (for members of religious communities)	2 (4%)	4	44 (96%)	20
Junior colleges (open to laymen)	2 (5%)	4	24 (69%)	11
Colleges (for members of religious communities)	3 (8%)	6	35 (92%)	15
Colleges (under 1,000 total enrollment)	12 (11%)	23	80 (74%)	36
Colleges (1,000 to 5,000 total enrollment)	27 (27%)	52	40 (39%)	18
Colleges (over 5,000 total enrollment)	6 (29%)	11		
TOTAL	52 (15%)	100	223 (64%)	100

SOURCE: *The 1967 Official Guide to Catholic Educational Institutions* and Marjorie O. Chandler and M. Rice, *Opening Fall Enrollment in Higher Education 1967* (U.S. Department of Health, Education, and Welfare, Washington, D.C., 1967), hereinafter referred to as *Opening Fall Enrollment in Higher Education 1967.*

Catholic higher educational institutions	Male		Female	
	Number	Percent	Number	Perce
Junior colleges (for members of religious communities)	210 (9%)	*	2,260 (91%)	2
Junior colleges (open to laymen)	204 (2%)	*	6,485 (60%)	6
Colleges (for members of religious communities)	927 (15%)	1	5,226 (85%)	5
Colleges (under 1,000 total enrollment)	7,692 (12%)	7	46,143 (71%)	42
Colleges (1,000 to 5,000 total enrollment)	61,052 (33%)	53	50,481 (28%)	45
Colleges (over 5,000 total enrollment)	44,094 (25%)	39		
TOTAL	114,179 (26%)	100	110,595 (25%)	100

*Less than 0.5 percent.

SOURCE: *The 1967 Official Guide to Catholic Educational Institutions* and *Opening Fall Enrollment in Higher Education 1967.*

Coed		Total	
mber	Percent	Number	Percent
		46 (100%)	13
9 .6%)	12	35 (100%)	10
		38 (100%)	11
6 5%)	21	108 (100%)	31
5 4%)	47	102 (100%)	29
5 1%)	20	21 (100%)	6
5 1%)	100	350 (100%)	100

Coed		Total	
mber	Percent	Number	Percent
		2,470 (100%)	1
,063 (38%)	2	10,752 (100%)	2
		6,153 (100%)	1
,141 (17%)	5	64,976 (100%)	15
,700 (39%)	32	183,233 (100%)	41
,781 (75%)	61	178,875 (100%)	40
,685 (49%)	100	446,459 (100%)	100

TABLE 5
Catholic higher
educational
institutions by
total opening
fall enrollment
of over 5,000 in
1967 and total
full-time
students
enrolled

Catholic higher educational institutions	Total enrollment	Full-time students
Loyola University (Chicago)	12,631	7,208
Marquette University	12,488	9,638
St. John's University (New York)	11,677	7,957
St. Louis University	10,678	7,685
Fordham University	10,450	7,897
University of Dayton	10,131	7,513
Boston College	9,724	8,118
De Paul University	9,457	4,994
Seton Hall University	9,367	4,897
University of Detroit	8,803	5,154
Villanova University	7,946	5,396
University of Notre Dame	7,723	7,408
Georgetown University	7,479	6,509
Duquesne University	6,874	4,909
St. Joseph's College (Philadelphia)	6,757	2,500
Catholic University of America	6,548	4,486
Catholic University of Puerto Rico	6,363	3,373
University of San Francisco	6,344	3,911
La Salle College (Philadelphia)	6,306	3,206
Xavier University (Cincinnati)	5,995	2,720
University of Santa Clara	5,114	3,432

SOURCE: *Opening Fall Enrollment in Higher Education 1967.*

TABLE 6
Enrollment in
Catholic higher
educational
institutions
by sex

Catholic higher educational institutions	Male	
	Number	Percen
Junior colleges (for members of religious communities)	210 (9%)	*
Junior colleges (open to laymen)	2,214 (21%)	1
Colleges (for members of religious communities)	927 (15%)	*
Colleges (under 1,000 total enrollment)	14,755 (23%)	6
Colleges (1,000 to 5,000 enrollment)	99,777 (54%)	41
Colleges (over 5,000 total enrollment)	127,886 (71%)	52
TOTAL	245,769 (55%)	100

*Less than 0.5 percent.

SOURCE: *The 1967 Official Guide to Catholic Educational Institutions* and *Opening Fall Enrollment in Higher Education 1967.*

of the country, and these schools enroll approximately 80 percent of all the students who are attending Catholic colleges. Furthermore, 16 of the 21 institutions having an enrollment of over 5,000 are in the same area, and if one adds Georgetown and The Catholic University of America in Washington, D.C., and the Catholic University of Puerto Rico (which is, to some considerable extent, an appendage of the New York Archdiocese), then 19 of the 21 large institutions containing 38 percent of the students are also found in the same region (Tables 7 and 8).

Finally, from Table 9 we note that 80 percent of the Catholic schools, 90 percent of the total enrollment, and all the colleges with over 5,000 students are found in standard metropolitan statistical areas.

Thus, while there are a large number of Catholic colleges and universities, the schools are, nonetheless, concentrated in the Northeast and North Central regions in the metropolitan statistical areas and are dominated in terms of enrollment by 21 institutions, all of which have more than 5,000 students and which together account for two-fifths of the young people currently receiving their higher education under the auspices of the Catholic Church.

Female		*Total*	
nber	*Percent*	*Number*	*Percent*
?60 (91%)	1	2,470 (100%)	1
?38 (79%)	4	10,752 (100%)	2
?26 (85%)	3	6,153 (100%)	1
?21 (77%)	25	64,976 (100%)	15
?56 (46%)	42	183,233 (100%)	41
?89 (29%)	25	178,875 (100%)	40
?0 (45%)	100	446,459 (100%)	100

TABLE 7 *Number of Catholic higher educational institutions by census regions*

Catholic higher educational institutions	New England			Middle Atlantic			East North Central			West North Central		
	Male	*Female*	*Coed*	*Male*	*Female*	*Coed*	*Male*	*Female*	*Coed*	*Male*	*Female*	*C...*
Junior colleges (for members of religious communities)		6		1	10			12			4	
Junior colleges (open to laymen)					13		1	2	1	1	3	
Colleges (for members of religious communities)	1	15			11		1	1			3	
Colleges (under 1,000 total enrollment)	1	14		1	22		3	14	6		12	
Colleges (1,000 to 5,000 total enrollment)	5	2	4	9	14	7	2	10	8	7	5	
Colleges (over 5,000 total enrollment)			1	4		3	2		5			
TOTAL	7	37	5	15	70	10	9	39	20	8	27	1

SOURCE: *The 1967 Official Guide to Catholic Educational Institutions.*

TABLE 8
Total enrollment in Catholic higher educational institutions by census regions

Catholic higher educational institutions	New England	Middle Atlantic	East North Central	West North Central	South Atlan...
Junior colleges (for members of religious communities)	217	631	687	164	20
Junior colleges (open to laymen)		3,583	1,247	3,018	1,62
Colleges (for members of religious communities)	2,066	1,563	117	826	86
Colleges (under 1,000 total enrollment)	8,136	13,312	13,444	7,782	5,00
Colleges (1,000 to 5,000 total enrollment)	21,708	58,929	31,658	23,736	7,57
Colleges (over 5,000 total enrollment)	9,724	59,377	67,248	10,678	14,02
TOTAL	41,851	137,395	114,401	46,204	29,30

SOURCE: *Opening Fall Enrollment in Higher Education 1967.*

		East South Central			West South Central			Mountain			Pacific			Outlying areas			Total		
	Coed	*Male*	*Female*	*Coed*	*Male*	*Female*	*Coed*	*Male*	*Female*	*Coed*	*Male*	*Female*	*Coed*	*Male*	*Female*	*Coed*	*Male*	*Female*	*Coed*
	2		1		4			1			4						2	44	
5			1	2		2											2	24	9
					2						3						3	35	
4	1		3	1	2	2		1	1	2	3	7	2		1		12	80	16
3	1	2	1	3	2	4			2		1	3	3				27	40	35
	2												2			1	6		15
4	4	2	6	6	10	8	1	2	4		4	17	7		1	1	52	223	75

	West South Central	Mountain	Pacific	Outlying areas	Total
38	108	21	396		2,470
27	756				10,752
	135		585		6,153
41	2,589	3,945	8,149	571	64,976
11	13,333	2,662	14,517		183,233
			11,458	6,363	178,875
17	16,921	6,628	35,105	6,934	446,459

TABLE 9
Catholic higher educational institutions by location in standard metropolitan statistical areas (SMSA)

Catholic higher educational institutions	In SMSA	Not in SMSA	Total
Junior college (for members of religious communities):			
Number	33	13	46
Total enrollment	1,908	562	2,470
Part-time enrollment	798	203	1,001
Percent part time	42%	36%	41%
Total staff	460	219	679
Part-time staff	267	123	390
Percent part time	58%	56%	57%
Junior colleges (open to laymen):			
Number	26	9	35
Total enrollment	8,488	2,264	10,752
Part-time enrollment	1,803	235	2,038
Percent part time	21%	10%	19%
Total staff	884	265	1,149
Part-time staff	326	90	416
Percent part time	37%	34%	36%
Colleges (for members of religious communities):			
Number	32	6	38
Total enrollment	5,728	425	6,153
Part-time enrollment	2,598	125	2,723
Percent part time	45%	29%	44%
Total staff	773	132	905
Part-time staff	382	39	421
Percent part time	49%	30%	47%
Colleges (under 1,000 total enrollment):			
Number	77	31	108
Total enrollment	48,310	16,666	64,976
Part-time enrollment	9,119	2,640	11,759
Percent part time	19%	16%	18%
Total staff	5,288	1,794	7,082
Part-time staff	1,499	427	1,926
Percent part time	28%	24%	27%

SOURCE: *The 1967 Official Guide to Catholic Educational Institutions* and *Opening Fall Enrollment in Higher Education 1967.*

Catholic higher educational institutions	In SMSA	Not in SMSA	Total
Colleges (1,000 to 5,000 total enrollment):			
Number	90	12	102
Total enrollment	164,608	18,625	183,233
Part-time enrollment	41,512	2,747	44,259
Percent part time	25%	15%	24%
Total staff	12,932	1,411	14,343
Part-time staff	3,257	247	3,504
Percent part time	25%	18%	24%
Colleges (over 5,000 total enrollment):			
Number	21		21
Total enrollment	178,875		178,875
Part-time enrollment	57,378		57,378
Percent part time	32%		32%
Total staff	14,655		14,655
Part-time staff	5,980		5,980
Percent part time	41%		41%
TOTAL:			
Number	279	71	350
Total enrollment	407,917	38,542	446,459
Part-time enrollment	113,208	5,950	119,158
Percent part time	28%	15%	27%
Total staff	34,992	3,821	38,813
Part-time staff	11,711	926	12,637
Percent part time	33%	24%	33%

SPONSORSHIP The nature of the relationship between Roman Catholic colleges and the sponsoring church is in transition. In almost all instances the legal ownership of the schools is vested in boards of trustees who, until very recently, were all members of the religious community that sponsored the school, or, in the case of the 24 "diocesan" colleges, in most instances the priests of the sponsoring diocese. The extent of the control exercised by the sponsoring institution, even before the recent change to partially or totally laicized boards of trustees, varied greatly.

The most important group of colleges is the 28 institutions run by the Society of Jesus which, even though they represent less than 10 percent of all the schools, enroll almost one-third of the students in Catholic higher education (Table 10). Jesuit schools are large—all but two of them have an enrollment over 1,000, and 11 of them have an enrollment over 5,000. Other religious orders of men sponsor 55 schools with 28 percent of the enrollment and include among their number St. John's University in New York,[1] probably the most notorious of the Catholic schools, and the University of Notre Dame in South Bend, probably the most famous. The majority of the schools have over 1,000 enrollment (29 between 1,000 and 5,000, and 7 over 5,000), though the other religious orders, unlike the Jesuits, do sponsor some relatively small colleges. The religious

---

[1] St. John's had dismissed more than a score of its faculty members in the middle of the academic year without anything resembling due process. Protests were launched both by the St. John's chapter to the AAUP and by the local chapter of the American Federation of Teachers. For well over a year St. John's adamantly refused all attempts at mediation. St. John's must be given due credit for the considerable improvement that has been made since the time of the famous strike. A layman has been appointed vice-president and a non-Catholic, provost. Tenure regulations typical of most American universities have become mandatory, faculty salaries have been dramatically increased, and the threat of discreditation by Middle States Accrediting Agency has been lifted. Nonetheless, the school is still under censure from the AAUP, and at the time of the present writing, the struggle between St. John's and the remnants of the strikers has not been satisfactorily resolved. In addition, at least some of the officials at St. John's are bent on continuing their past attitudes. Thus, in a previous volume the present writer had one paragraph which alluded to newspaper accounts of the controversy of the university. One member of St. John's administration wrote three particularly vicious letters to the publisher of the volume to attempt to prevent publication on the grounds that the newspaper accounts were unfair to St. John's and that a reference to the newspaper accounts was not proper. The Spring, 1969, issue of the AAUP *Bulletin* noted that the changes at St. John's were not yet completely reassuring.

TABLE 10 *Catholic higher educational institutions by control* (dollars in thousands)

Catholic higher educational institutions	Dioceses*	Society of Jesus	Orders of men	Orders of women	Total
Junior colleges (religious):					
Number	2		2	42	46
Enrollment	94		100	2,276	2,470
Federal support				$ 20	$ 20
Junior colleges (laymen):					
Number	1		3	31	35
Enrollment	958		768	9,026	10,752
Federal support	$ 28		$ 26	$ 1,133	$ 1,187
Colleges (religious):					
Number	3		1	34	38
Enrollment	804		861	4,488	6,153
Federal support				$ 214	$ 214
Colleges (under 1,000):					
Number	4	2	13	89	108
Enrollment	2,554	1,812	9,384	51,226	64,976
Federal support	$ 262	$ 270	$ 2,643	$ 11,392	$ 14,567
Colleges (1,000 - 5,000):					
Number	9	15	29	49	102
Enrollment	16,820	45,902	57,909	62,602	183,233
Federal support	$ 1,296	$ 9,535	$ 11,457	$ 12,316	$ 34,604
Colleges (over 5,000):					21
Number	3	11	7		178,875
Enrollment	22,278	96,483	60,114		$ 73,015
Federal support	6,898	$48,677	$ 17,440		
TOTAL					
Number	22	28	55	245	350
Enrollment	43,508	144,197	129,136	129,618	446,459
Federal support	$ 8,484	$ 58,482	$ 31,566	$ 25,075	$123,607

*Includes Catholic University of America and other institutions not affiliated with particular orders.

SOURCE: *The 1967 Official Guide to Catholic Educational Institutions, Opening Fall Enrollment in Higher Education 1967* and National Science Foundation for the Office of Science and Technology, *Federal Support for Academic Science and Other Educational Activities in Universities and Colleges, Fiscal Years 1963 - 66* (National Science Foundation, Washington, 1967).

orders of women, on the other hand, have, as one might expect, the overwhelmingly largest block of schools—245—though they enroll fewer students in those schools than the Jesuits do in their 28. The "diocesan" category is the smallest both in number of schools (22) and in enrollment (11 percent), but it does include

TABLE 11   *Teacher and administrative staff at Catholic institutions of higher education*

Catholic institutions of higher education	Full time				Part time	
	Religious		Lay		Religious	
	Number	Percent	Number	Percent	Number	Percent
Junior colleges (for members of religious communities)	289	1	8	3	390	3
Junior colleges (open to laymen)	733	3	276	38	416	3
Colleges (for members of religious communities)	484	2	19	4	421	3
Colleges (under 1,000 total enrollment)	5,156	20	2,154	42	1,926	15
Colleges (1,000 to 5,000 total enrollment)	10,839	41	6,431	59	3,504	28
Colleges (over 5,000 total enrollment)	8,675	33	7,046	81	5,980	48
TOTAL	26,176	100	15,934	61	12,637	100

SOURCE: *The 1967 Official Guide to Catholic Educational Institutions* and *Opening Fall Enrollment in Higher Education 1967.*

some major institutions, such as The Catholic University of America in Washington and the Catholic University in Puerto Rico.[2]

We note once again, then, the vast diversity of Catholic higher

[2] The 22 "diocesan," etc. schools:

Junior colleges, religious: St. Theresa's Institute, Philadelphia, Pennsylvania; Villa Walsh College, Morristown, New Jersey.

Lay: Donnelly College, Kansas City, Kansas.

Colleges, religious: Catholic Teachers College of Providence, Rhode Island; Maryglade College, Memphis, Michigan; St. Basil's College, Stamford, Connecticut.

Under 1,000: St. Mary's College, Orchard Lake, Michigan; Carroll College, Helena, Montana; Mount St. Mary's College, Emmitsburg, Maryland; University of San Diego—College for Men;

1,000-5,000: Gannon College, Erie, Pennsylvania; Villa Madonna College, Covington, Kentucky; University of Dallas, Dallas, Texas; Bellarmine College, Louisville, Kentucky; St. Ambrose College, Davenport, Iowa; Loras College, Dubuque, Iowa; College of St. Thomas, St. Paul, Minnesota; St. John College of Cleveland, Cleveland, Ohio; Sacred Heart University, Bridgeport, Connecticut.

Over 5,000: Catholic University of Puerto Rico; The Catholic University of America; Seton Hall University.

Lay		Total				Percent part time	Total student-faculty rating
		Religious		Lay			
nber	*Percent*	*Number*	*Percent*	*Number*	*Percent*	*time*	*rating*
38	10	679	2	46	7	57	3.6
08	50	1,149	3	484	42	36	9.4
0	19	905	2	99	11	47	6.8
8	53	7,082	18	3,172	45	27	9.2
3	78	14,343	37	9,174	64	24	12.8
0	96	14,655	38	12,776	87	41	12.2
7	78	38,813	100	25,751	66	33	11.5

education combined with strong concentration in certain schools. The 28 Jesuit institutions must clearly be considered the dominating "block" within the "system." If this block were well organized and systematically coordinated, it would be able to dominate the rest of the "system." However, it would be a mistake to think that the fact that these 28 schools are all sponsored by the Society of Jesus means that they have common policy and make common decisions. The American branch of the Society of Jesus is divided into 11 provinces.[3] Cooperation across provincial lines is not highly developed, and even within a given province the two or three Jesuit schools under one provincial may frequently be competing with one another for personnel and resources when cooperating. Certain common policy decisions are made at the occasional meetings of the Jesuit college presidents or of the provincials, and an attempt is made to coordinate operations through the offices of the Jesuit

[3] At the present time the provincial structure is being rearranged in such a way as to lead to a decrease in the number of provinces.

Educational Association in Washington. But the JEA's staff is small and its power almost nonexistent, save insofar as its president is able to exercise power by his personal influence.[4] There is little

[4] The current president, Paul Reinert of the University of St. Louis, does have considerable personal influence because of his own successful administration of the St. Louis university.

TABLE 12
Estimated number of employed personnel by primary function in Catholic institutions of higher education, fall, 1966

Primary function and status of employed personnel	Full time		Part time	
	Number	Percent	Number	Percen
Resident instruction and departmental research				
Professional personnel				
Senior staff	21,903	45	8,879	29
Junior staff	583	1	2,381	8
Nonprofessional personnel	2,224	5	2,972	10
Organized research				
Professional personnel				
Senior staff	335	1	163	1
Junior staff	367	1	670	2
Nonprofessional personnel	430	1	326	1
Library				
Professional personnel				
Professional librarians	912	2	174	1
Other professional	310	1	66	*
Nonprofessional personnel	995	2	2,879	10
Extension and public service				
Professional personnel				
For formal instruction	91	*	537	2
For consultation	24	*	55	*
Other	24	*	11	*
Nonprofessional personnel	97	*	21	*
Auxiliary enterprises				
Professional personnel	605	1	110	*
Nonprofessional personnel	6,442	13	5,155	17
Schools operated				
Professional personnel				
Elementary schools	99	*	35	*
Secondary schools	146	*	29	*
Nonprofessional personnel	74	*	92	*
All other employed personnel				
Professional personnel	2,861	6	464	1
Nonprofessional personnel	9,825	21	5,285	18
TOTAL	48,347	100	30,304	100

*Less than 0.5 percent.
SOURCE: Carnegie Commission on Higher Education tabulation based on U.S. Office of Education data.

exchange of faculty or administrative staff among the Jesuit schools, particularly beyond provincial lines; and a number of close observers of American higher education have noted that in many instances Jesuit schools have far more in common with other Catholic institutions that are not Jesuit than they do with certain other schools run by Jesuit colleagues. Thus in the new and still informal

E of part time		Total		Total FTE	
ber	*Percent*	*Number*	*Percent*	*Number*	*Percent*
¡99	34	30,782	39	25,302	43
¡59	9	2,964	4	1,542	3
¡70	8	5,216	7	3,094	5
64	1	498	1	399	1
¡43	2	1,037	1	610	1
38	1	756	1	568	1
49	1	1,086	1	961	2
22	*	376	1	332	1
¡58	8	3,874	5	1,853	3
¡45	1	628	1	236	*
16	*	79	*	40	*
2	*	35	*	26	*
7	*	118	*	104	*
34	*	715	1	639	1
¡74	16	11,597	15	8,116	14
13	*	134	*	112	*
13	*	175	*	159	*
48	1	166	*	122	*
¡19	1	3,325	4	2,951	5
¡18	17	15,110	19	11,543	20
391	100	78,651	100	58,738	100

grouping of American Catholic universities, Boston College and Fordham are in themselves allied with Notre Dame[5] to the exclusion of certain other Jesuit schools which might feel that they have a legitimate claim to be a university but are not, in fact, welcomed into the inner circle. Therefore, the heavy concentration of students in the Jesuit schools does not give the Jesuits a "stranglehold" in American higher education. The size of the Jesuit enrollment does, of course, allow them considerable influence, but it is a diffuse and uncoordinated influence, not a monolithic and irresistible one.

[5] This alliance was nominally the American Branch of the International Federation of Catholic Universities, of which Notre Dame's Father Theodore Hesburgh was president.

TABLE 13
Distribution of reported faculty degrees in Catholic institutions of higher education (full time and part time)

Catholic institutions of higher education	Doctors		Masters	
	Number	Percent	Number	Perce
Junior colleges (for members of religious communities)	85 (16%)	1	314 (61%)	?
Junior colleges (open to laymen)	105 (12%)	1	575 (66%)	*
Colleges (for members of religious communities)	157 (21%)	2	485 (66%)	?
Colleges (under 1,000 total enrollment)	1,480 (26%)	16	3,329 (58%)	2?
Colleges (1,000 to 5,000 total enrollment)	3,443 (29%)	36	6,437 (55%)	4?
Colleges (over 5,000 total enrollment)	4,214 (39%)	44	3,677 (34%)	2?
TOTAL	9,484 (31%)	100	14,817 (49%)	10?

*Less than 0.5 percent.
SOURCE: *The 1967 Official Guide to Catholic Educational Institutions.*

FACULTY AND ADMINISTRA-TION Even though the schools are still more or less sponsored by religious orders or by dioceses, they are increasingly becoming staffed by lay-men. Although there are only a few lay presidents in the Catholic "system" and a few more lay vice-presidents (the minority of these would be academic vice-presidents or "provosts") almost every major institution has a number of lay deans, and three-fifths of the full-time faculty and almost eight-tenths of the part-time faculty are lay (Table 11). The smaller the school, the more likely the faculty is to be composed for the most part of members of religious orders, though even in the schools with under 1,000 enrollment, two-fifths of the full-time teachers are laymen. As one may expect, also, the use of part-time teachers is most likely to occur at the largest institutions.

Bachelors		Professional and other		Total	
mber	Percent	Number	Percent	Number	Percent
04 (20%)	3	14 (3%)	1	517 (100%)	2
72 (20%)	5	20 (2%)	1	872 (100%)	3
86 (12%)	2	9 (1%)	*	737 (100%)	2
58 (13%)	20	151 (3%)	6	5,718 (3%)	19
95 (13%)	40	309 (3%)	13	11,684 (100%)	38
25 (10%)	30	1,894 (17%)	79	10,910 (100%)	36
40 (12%)	100	2,397 (8%)	100	30,438 (100%)	100

On a full-time employment basis, the professional personnel engaged in resident instruction and departmental research account for 46 percent of all employed personnel (Table 12).

While it is peculiarly difficult even to define what the Catholic school faculty member is, much less to measure his skill, it must be noted that in terms of earned degrees, Catholic schools have a large number of trained staff members. There are over 9,400 Ph.D.s teaching in Catholic higher education. When the more than 2,000 faculty members with professional degrees are added to these, it can be seen that approximately two-fifths of the full- or part-time faculty members of the Catholic colleges and universities do have terminal degrees in their disciplines (Table 13). In evaluating these proportions, it must be kept in mind that, since relatively few Catholic institutions offer comprehensive graduate programs, the teaching assistant is a relatively rare phenomenon in Catholic higher education. Positions occupied by TAs in other universities are, in the Catholic schools, to a considerable extent

TABLE 14
Estimated characteristics of faculty and staff (full time only) in Catholic institutions of higher education, fall, 1966

Rank of full-time faculty	Bachelor's degrees or lower		Selected first profession degrees	
	Number	*Percent*	*Number*	*Perce*
Academic dean	9	2	32	
Percent				3
Professor	66	2	239	
Percent		3		21
Associate professor	98	2	204	
Percent		4		18
Assistant professor	369	5	364	
Percent		16		31
Instructor	1,040	17	223	
Percent		45		19
Junior staff	599	83	27	
Percent		26		2
Other/no rank	145	18	71	
Percent		6		6
TOTAL	2,326	10	1,160	
Percent		100		100

occupied by Ph.D. candidates, most of whom are still actively doing their degree work, probably at a large non-Catholic university in the same city or very near the school at which they are teaching.

As one would expect, the proportion of those with higher degrees is highest at large institutions, where more than half of the faculty members possess such degrees. However, the differential is not great; 39 percent of the faculty members in colleges with over 5,000 students have Ph.D.'s, as do 26 percent of those at the small schools with under 1,000 students. Further, while at the large institutions 10 percent of the teachers have only A.B. degrees, the proportion for colleges under 1,000 is only three percentage points higher. No claim could be made, of course, that the faculties of the Catholic institutions have the kind of training that would permit most of them to be on the staffs of the best American universities. Nevertheless, in terms of degrees, Catholic schools are by no means complete wastelands.

Table 14 provides data only for faculty members employed full-

Master's degrees		Doctor's degrees		Total	
ber	*Percent*	*Number*	*Percent*	*Number*	*Percent*
165	31	327	61	533	100
	1		4		2
879	22	2,768	70	3,952	100
	7		35		17
863	43	2,192	50	4,357	100
	16		27		19
985	58	2,165	32	6,883	100
	34		27		30
416	73	361	6	6,040	100
	37		5		26
81	11	13	2	720	100
	1				3
422	52	178	22	816	100
	4		2		3
311	51	8,004	34	23,301	100
	100		100		100

time. It shows that 34 percent of these faculty members in all ranks, or 47 percent of the professors alone, hold the doctorate. The professorial ranks make up 66 percent of the full-time faculty.

Further analysis of the full-time and part-time faculty members in Catholic colleges and universities is provided in Table 15. It indicates that although these institutions enroll only a little more than 6½ percent of the nation's students in higher education, they have 7 percent of the full-time and 8 percent of the part-time faculty in the country. Thus there are slightly more faculty members per

TABLE 15 *Estimated number of full-time and part-time faculty in Catholic institutions of higher education by major area of teaching and/or research, fall, 1966*

Major area of teaching and/or research	Professors		Associate professors		Assistant professors	
	Full time	Part time	Full time	Part time	Full time	Part time
Agriculture and related fields					1	
Architecture	9		7		11	
Biological sciences	273	19	255	18	348	
Business and commerce	211	13	291	25	409	
Education and related fields	260	44	289	27	424	
Engineering	108	4	139	7	185	
English and journalism	389	39	403	40	695	
Fine and applied arts	182	31	330	31	427	
Foreign languages and literature	411	44	346	34	614	
Geography	4	2	6	2	8	
Health professions	184	132	256	285	533	50
Home economics	16	2	38	1	44	
Law	148	62	47	7	52	
Library science	81	72	43	5	26	
Mathematics	154	11	168	19	378	
Military science	49		10		188	
Philosophy	351	32	276	15	410	
Physical and health education	10		55	3	127	
Physical sciences	380	25	263	24	504	
Psychology	103	15	124	11	192	
Religion and theology	434	63	214	37	379	
Social sciences	526	43	582	34	822	
Trade and industrial	3		5	1	5	
All other fields	226	3	232	4	440	
TOTAL	4,512	656	4,379	630	7,222	1,0
Percent of total United States	7	10	7	11	8	

SOURCE: Carnegie Commission on Higher Education tabulation based on U.S. Office of Education data.

student in Catholic colleges and universities than in the rest of American higher education. These data also affirm the previously noted fact that Catholic institutions depend on senior staff to a greater degree than non-Catholic institutions do.

An examination of the number of faculty members in the various disciplines (also in Table 15) shows a concentration of full professors in religion and theology that is second only to the number in the social sciences, which might be a good indication of where the power lies in Catholic institutions. Also, it is only in religion and

tructors	*Junior staff*		*Other academic faculty*		*Total*		*Percent total U.S.*	
Part time	*Full time*	*Part time*	*Full time*	*Part time*	*Full time*	*Part time*	*Full time*	*Part time*
1					2	1		
1	1	1	1	13	28	14	2	2
84	63	146	13	103	1,209	389	6	5
201	12	114	12	569	1,213	954	7	9
219	15	76	28	335	1,307	751	6	9
13	2	53	8	117	496	198	3	2
214	35	224	30	222	2,276	793	8	8
345	11	85	24	355	1,477	897	5	8
225	37	81	31	223	2,133	639	13	9
14		2		12	32	33	2	4
860	115	190	16	862	1,615	2,831	6	12
27		7		12	148	52	4	3
11	1	17		108	256	208	10	16
20			10	32	188	133	12	23
135	31	98	12	131	1,116	418	7	5
1	11		26	13	359	15	14	8
61	14	64	41	124	1,497	328	30	23
78	2	34	8	51	367	187	3	6
117	102	238	30	129	1,558	555	6	4
76	11	88	4	133	540	358	7	7
259	7	52	53	201	1,630	686	31	36
268	80	133	39	389	2,705	922	8	7
4			1	2	31	8	1	
51	218	17	26	194	1,338	271	19	6
3,285	767	1,719	412	4,330	23,521	11,641	7	8
9	4	3	2	16	7	8		

TABLE 16
Estimated salaries of full-time faculty, fall, 1966, in Catholic institutions of higher education

Salary intervals	Academic deans 9-10 months	Academic deans 11-12 months	Professors 9-10 months	Professors 11-12 months	Associate professors 9-10 months	Associate professors 11 mo
$36,000 and over		1				
35,000-35,999						
34,000-34,999						
33,000-33,999						
32,000-32,999						
31,000-31,999						
30,000-30,999		1				
29,000-29,999		1				
28,000-28,999		1				
27,000-27,999						
26,000-26,999	1	1				
25,000-25,999		3	2			
24,000-24,999	1	6		1		
23,000-23,999		4	4	3		
22,000-22,999	3	4	3	1		
21,000-21,999		3	3	3		
20,000-20,999	3	11	11	4		
19,000-19,999	2	4	5	8		
18,000-18,999	1	3	13	18	1	
17,000-17,999	3	11	25	22		
16,000-16,999	1	13	41	26	8	
15,000-15,999	6	21	131	44	20	
14,000-14,999	3	12	124	46	21	
13,000-13,999	2	20	169	82	54	
12,000-12,999	7	20	258	82	155	
11,000-11,999		6	255	44	306	
10,000-10,999	3	5	228	60	465	
9,000-9,999	6	6	149	14	600	
8,000-8,999	2	15	55	5	387	
7,000-7,999	3	18	54	1	180	
6,000-6,999	2	1	31	3	56	
5,000-5,999		1	20	6	17	
4,000-4,999			2	4	1	
Under $4,000	5		66	53	9	
TOTAL Salaried	54	192	1,649	530	2,280	
Nonsalaried	99	178	1,183	495	987	2,4
Percent nonsalaried personnel	65%	48%	42%	48%	30%	
Percent distribution		53%		44%		55%
Salaried personnel		2%		15%		19%
Nonsalaried personnel		3%		19%		37%

*Less than 0.5 percent.

SOURCE: Carnegie Commission on Higher Education tabulation based on U.S. Office of Education data.

	Assistant professors		Instructors		Junior staff		Other academic faculty		Total	
	...hs months	11-12 months	9-10 months	11-12 months	9-10 months	11-12 months	9-10 months	11-12 months	9-10 months	11-12 months
										1
										1
										1
										1
									1	1
									2	3
									1	7
									4	7
									6	5
									3	6
									14	15
									7	14
									15	25
									28	36
	1								15	41
1	1	7						1	158	98
1	1	7		1				1	148	90
	8	19		1				1	233	156
	4	33					3	2	437	189
7	7	42	3	5	1		1	4	623	153
7	7	78	9	14			3	7	955	286
5	5	110	26	19	2		2	7	1,510	246
3	3	164	222	53	8		7	8	1,964	325
2	2	119	959	125	13		18	12	2,459	307
6	6	63	1,733	184	57	3	18	11	2,263	269
1	1	12	422	52	32	3	18	12	570	87
0	0	2	64	22	81	1	7	9	175	39
5	5	1	69	9	231	49	103	23	498	136
0		658	3,507	484	425	56	180	98	12,125	2,545
1		518	1,229	445	13	8	139	113	4,991	4,172
...5%		44%	26%	48%	3%	13%	44%	54%	29%	62%
		28%		30%		4%		48%		38%
		32%		27%		3%		2%	100%	
		20%		18%		*		3%	100%	

theology that the number of full professors in Catholic institution:
is greater than either associate or assistant professors.

It is extremely difficult both to judge the level of faculty salar;
in Catholic colleges and universities and to estimate the teaching
loads. According to the most recent AAUP report, 10 Catholi
schools[6] have a B rating in faculty salary, 38 have a C rating, 3(
have a D rating, and four have an E rating.[7] However, by no mean:
all the Catholic colleges have reported their faculty salaries. O:
those reporting, 60 percent rate C or better, while 64 percent o
all the institutions rated by the AAUP rank C or better. These
figures would suggest that at least among the reporting school:
the salary picture of the Catholic schools is not much differen
from the average, though Catholic schools are not found in the
A category (but neither are 96 percent of the rest of the school:
in the country). A few schools have announced that they intend to
pay at the A level, but they have yet to achieve the goal. On the
other hand, at lower faculty levels a number of Catholic school:
have already achieved A status and many more are in the B cate
gory. The upgrading has begun with the junior faculty, both, i
would seem, because of the competition for younger faculty mem
bers and also because the junior faculty member probably has more
academic training and better professional orientation than doe:
the older faculty member.

There has also been a major shift in recent years in the teaching
loads. Although no exact figures are available, it was the impression
of the NORC staff during their study of Catholic colleges that a
the small liberal arts colleges the teaching load was now usually
12 hours; at the medium-sized colleges and the smaller and les:
prestigious universities the teaching load was 9 hours, though there
was a tendency for an increasing number of faculty members, par
ticularly if they were doing research, to teach only 6 hours. At the

[6] Fordham, Boston College, Santa Clara, The Catholic University of America
Georgetown, Notre Dame, St. John's (Minnesota), Holy Cross, Marquette, anc
St. Mary's (California).

[7] In the AAUP *Bulletin,* December, 1968 (winter issue), the following average
compensation scale was published:

	AA	A	B	C	D	E	F
Professor	$28,490	$22,680	$17,940	$14,350	$11,500	$9,500	$ 8,44
Associate Prof.	16,350	14,240	12,560	10,970	9,500	8,340	7,60
Assistany Prof.	12,660	11,290	10,090	9,050	8,190	7,490	6,96
Instructor	9,500	8,760	8,100	7,530	7,050	6,650	6,33

TABLE 17 *Libraries in Catholic institutions of higher education*

Catholic institutions of higher education	Volumes		Average size	Volumes per student
	Number	Percent		
Junior colleges (for members of religious communities)	554,394	2	12,320	224
Junior colleges (open to laymen)	609,924	3	17,426	57
Colleges (for members of religious communities)	814,536	4	22,626	132
Colleges (under 1,000 total enrollment)	4,899,622	21	45,367	75
Colleges (1,000 to 5,000 total enrollment)	8,381,570	36	82,172	46
Colleges (over 5,000 total enrollment)	7,778,615	34	370,410	43
TOTAL	23,038,661	100	65,825	52

SOURCE: *The 1967 Official Guide to Catholic Educational Institutions* and *Opening Fall Enrollment in Higher Education 1967.*

major institutions, such as the University of Notre Dame, a six-hour teaching load was becoming normative.

Thirty-eight percent of all full-time faculty (Table 16) are nonsalaried by the institutions. (This proportion probably includes those who contribute services, plus ROTC faculty members who are paid by the Department of Defense, plus those on sabbatical.) Forty-four percent of the professors and 55 percent of the associate professors are nonsalaried. Generally, the nonsalaried personnel hold higher ranks than the salaried. The salaries themselves are hard to describe except that they do have quite a range (and the larger institutions pay higher salaries at all ranks), and, in total, appear to be low.

LIBRARIES   Complaints about the inadequacy of library facilities are widespread in Catholic higher education. Table 17 shows that there are 52 books for every student in Catholic higher education, though the ratio of books per student is much better in the smaller schools than it is in the larger ones.[8]

DEGREES CONFERRED   Table 18 shows the academic degrees conferred in Catholic colleges in 1966: there were 52,000 A.B.'s, almost 9,000 M.A.'s, and 506

[8] In all higher educational institutions in the United States, the number of books per student is approximately 42.

TABLE 18 **Academic** **degrees** **conferred in** **1966 by Catholic** **institutions of** **higher education**	*Catholic* *institutions* *of higher* *education*	*Bachelor's*		
		Degrees		*Conferring* *institutions*

Catholic institutions of higher education	*Number*	*Percent*	*Number*	*Perce*
Colleges (for members of religious communities)	734	1	23	9
Colleges (under 1,000 total enrollment)	9,378	18	103	42
Colleges (1,000 to 5,000 total enrollment)	22,989	44	100	40
Colleges (over 5,000 total enrollment)	19,338	37	21	9
TOTAL	52,439	100	247	100

*Less than 0.5 percent.
SOURCE: *The 1967 Official Guide to Catholic Educational Institutions.*

TABLE 19 **Catholic** **institutions of** **higher education** **conferring** **doctorates, 1966**	

Catholic institutions of higher education	*Number*
University of San Diego—College for Men	12
University of Portland	8
St. Bonaventure University	3
St. Mary's College (Notre Dame, Indiana)	1
St. John's University	30
Loyola University (Chicago)	32
Marquette University	10
Catholic University of America	135
Georgetown University	46
St. Louis University	59
University of Notre Dame	81
University of Detroit	1
Seton Hall University	14
Fordham University	45
Duquesne University	7
Boston College	22

SOURCE: *The 1967 Official Guide to Catholic Educational Institutions.*

	Master's				Doctor's		
	Degrees		Conferring institutions		Degrees		Conferring institutions
·er	Percent	Number	Percent	Number	Percent	Number	Percent
	*	1	1				
	2	13	17	12	2	1	6
	29	45	57	12	2	3	19
	69	20	25	482	96	12	75
	100	79	100	506	100	16	100

doctorates. Twelve institutions conferred 96 percent of the Ph.D.'s, and 20 institutions conferred seven-tenths of the M.A.'s.[9]

Table 19 lists the doctorates conferred by Catholic universities in 1966. The Catholic University of America leads the way with 135, and only four others—Notre Dame, St. Louis, Georgetown, and Fordham—awarded more than 40 doctorates. All in all, the doctorate-conferring institutions granted 2.8 percent of the doctorates conferred in the United States in 1966.

STUDENTS Table 20 shows that 119,158 of the students in the Catholic colleges or about 27 percent are part-time students, and that more than 85,000 students are first-time freshmen.[10] One is moved to ask who

[9] It is clear from this table that the principal emphasis of the Catholic colleges still is on the A.B. degree, and, as far as doctorate-level graduate training is concerned, Philip Gleason is quite right when he said that Catholic institutions became involved in this work "only yesterday."

[10] The statements in this paragraph are based on tables presented in *The Changing Catholic College* by the present author, William Van Cleve, and Grace Ann Carroll, and describe the June, 1961, Catholic graduates. More recent data of detail reported in the text are not available.

TABLE 20
Part-time enrollment and first-time freshman enrollment at Catholic institutions of higher education

Catholic institutions of higher education	Part-time enrollment		Perce of tot enrol
	Number	*Percent*	
Junior colleges (for members of religious communities)	1,001	1	41
Junior colleges (open to laymen)	2,038	2	19
Colleges (for members of religious communities)	2,723	2	44
Colleges (under 1,000 total enrollment)	11,759	10	18
Colleges (1,000 to 5,000 total enrollment)	44,259	37	24
Colleges (over 5,000 total enrollment)	57,378	48	32
TOTAL	119,158	100	27

SOURCE: *The 1967 Official Guide to Catholic Educational Institutions* an *Opening Enrollment in Higher Education 1967.*

TABLE 21
Undergraduate enrollment in Catholic higher educational institutions by race

Race	Fall 1967 enrollment		All U.S. colleges, percent	Catholic, percent of U.S. total
	Number	*Percent*		
White	274,370	96	92	6
Negro	5,567	2	5	2
Other	5,609	2	3	4
TOTAL	285,546	100	100	6

SOURCE: "White, Negro Undergraduates at Colleges Enrolling 500 or More, a Compiled from Reports to U.S. Office for Civil Rights," *The Chronicle of Highe Education,* Vol. 11, No. 16 (Apr. 22, 1968).

these young people are. Socially and demographically (Table 21), a typical graduate of a Catholic college or university is not very different from a typical American college graduate, though he is rather more different from his coreligionist who attended a non Catholic college. A Catholic college graduate is as likely to be a girl (43 percent), to come from a family where both parents went to college, as is a typical American college graduate (about two-fifths of the graduates' parents also attended college). Furthermore, the

| *rst-time freshman enrollment* | |
Number	Percent of total enrollment
ot available	
4,480	42
Jot available	
5,766	24
8,994	21
7,827	16

graduate of a Catholic college is just as likely as the Protestant graduate to come from a family whose income was over $7,500 a year and whose father was a professional man or manager. On the other hand, a Catholic who attended a non-Catholic college is much less likely to be a girl (only 31 percent) and probably comes from a smaller city and a distinctly lower socioeconomic background (only one-fifth of the fathers of the Catholics who went to non-Catholic colleges had themselves gone to college). Furthermore, almost one-third of the Catholics who went to non-Catholic colleges were either married or planning marriage before the fall after graduation (a proportion about the same as for Protestants who graduated from college), but only one-fifth of the graduates of Catholic colleges were either married or contemplating immediate marriage.

The graduates of Catholic colleges were also considerably more likely to be from the area north of the Mason-Dixon line and east of the Mississippi River, with 89 percent coming from this area, while only 68 percent of the Catholics who went to non-Catholic colleges were from this area. It is well worth noting that better than one-third of the graduates of Catholic colleges came from the five states of the old Northwest Territory—Illinois, Indiana, Michigan, Ohio, and Wisconsin. One of the most important facts about the graduates of Catholic colleges is that almost two-fifths of them were of Irish ancestry while approximately one-fifth of the proportion of Catholic graduates of non-Catholic colleges were Irish. In comparison with the Irish, all other backgrounds were slightly underrepresented among graduates of Catholic colleges. Other data indicate that 37 percent Irish in the 1961 graduating population represents a substantial decline in proportion of past graduation classes. Among Catholic adults who went to college, almost one-half had an Irish ancestral background. It is no secret, of course, that the Irish, because of their early arrival, knowledge of the language, and political skills, have been a dominant ethnic group within the American Church. It is also no secret that the Irish have traditionally been extremely loyal to Catholic institutions. Both because of organizational loyalty and organizational control, it is not unexpected that Catholic higher education is so heavily an Irish phenomenon.

In summary, then, the graduates of Catholic colleges are not different from typical American college graduates in socioeconomic background, though they are different in that they are less likely to marry either during college or shortly after college graduation.

AVERAGE CHARACTER-ISTICS Table 22 gives the average characteristics of the various categories of Catholic colleges. The "large" Catholic college (which, as we said, is one of the groups that enrolls 40 percent of the students) is not large compared with the major state universities. It has 8,500 students of whom 2,700 are part-time and 1,300 are first-time freshmen; 6,000 of the students are male; it has 698 faculty members, 413 of whom are full-time (and 336 of these are laymen), 285 part-time (of which 273 are laymen). This mythical typical school has 201 faculty members with Ph.D.'s, 175 with M.A.'s, 54 with only A.B. degrees, and another 91 who have professional degrees. In the previous year, it awarded 921 A.B.'s, 309 masters, and 40 Ph.D.'s; it has in its library 370,000 books. It is not a University of California at Berkeley or an Ohio State University either in size, resources, or complexity, but neither can it be written off as a minor and unimportant part of American higher education.

FINANCES The most striking phenomenon in Table 23 on current fund revenues is that the Catholic higher educational institutions re-

TABLE 22 *Average characteristics of Catholic institutions of higher education*

Characteristics	Junior colleges (for religious communities)	Junior colleges (open to laymen)	Colleges (for religious communities)	Colleges (less than 1,000)	Colleges (1,000-5,000)	Colleges (over 5,000)
Enrollment:						
Total	54	307	166	602	1,796	8,518
Male		64		138	978	6,048
Female		243		464	818	2,470
Part time	22	58	72	108	434	2,726
First-time freshmen	Not available	128	Not available	144	382	1,363
Faculty:						
Total	14	33	24	66	141	698
Full time	6	21	13	48	106	413
Full time (lay)		8	1	20	63	336
Part time	8	12	11	18	34	285
Part time (lay)	1	6	2	9	27	273
Doctors	2	3	4	14	34	201
Masters	7	16	13	31	63	175
Bachelors	2	5	2	7	15	54
Professional or other		1		1	3	91
Degrees conferred:						
Bachelor's			32	91	230	921
Master's						309
Doctor's						40
Library volumes	12,320	17,426	22,626	45,367	82,172	370,410

SOURCE: *The 1967 Official Guide to Catholic Educational Institutions* and *Opening Fall Enrollments in Higher Education 1967.*

ceive almost half (48 percent) of their incomes from tuition and fees, while other American private higher educational institutions get only 34 percent of their revenue from this source. Similarly, Catholic schools receive 6 percent of their current fund revenues from the federal government (most of which goes for organized research), compared to about one-quarter of the revenue of all private higher educational institutions. The principal difference between Catholic and other private higher educational institutions is organized research, with only 6 percent of Catholic revenue coming

TABLE 23
Estimated
current fund
revenues of
Catholic
institutions of
higher education
by purpose and
source, fiscal
year 1965-66
*(dollars in
thousands)*

| | Purpose | | | |
| | Educational and general | | | |
Source	All except organized research and organized activities	Organized research	Organized activities relating to educational departments	Stud. aid gran
Total current funds:				
Revenues	$450,448	$41,745	$20,796	$19,8
Tuition and fees	319,608	209	2,927	6,7
Room, board, and all other charges to individual users of services	1,768		3,093	5.
Earnings from endowment investment	10,756	105	138	2,1
Private gifts and grants	91,917	5,367	1,079	6,5
Local government	128	135	66	
State government	2,915	437	6	1,0
Federal government	7,052	33,410	1,465	2,6
Other sources	16,304	2,082	12,022	2
Percent distribution of Catholic total	65%	6%	3%	
Percent distribution of total United States	57	19	5	
Percent distribution of United States private	52	23	5	
Percent of total United States	6	2	3	
Percent of United States private	16	3	8	

SOURCE: Carnegie Commission on Higher Education tabulation from U.S. Office of Education data.

from organized research, whereas 23 percent of the revenue for all private higher educational institutions comes from organized research. Another way of looking at the matter is to say that Catholic higher educational institutions get slightly less than their "share" of total current fund revenues, much less from federal funds and much more in private gifts and grants. Catholic schools *uxiliary enterprises*

ousing nd food rvice	All other	Total	Percent distribution			Percent of	
			Total Catholic	Total U.S.	U.S. private	Total U.S.	U.S. private
17,394	$41,241	$691,517	100	100	100	5	13
141	1,162	330,805	48	22	34	12	18
13,408	24,603	143,392	21	16	17	7	16
41	73	13,237	2	3	6	4	4
1,909	625	107,413	15	6	10	15	20
		329		2			4
		4,372	1	24	2		5
65	27	44,690	6	22	25	2	3
1,830	14,751	47,279	7	5	6	7	14
17%	6%	100%					
10	7	100					
11	6	100					
9	5	5					
19	13	13					

have 6.5 percent of the total enrollment, only 2 percent of research funds, 5 percent of total current revenue, only 2 percent of the revenue from federal sources, but about 6 percent of student-aid grants. Surprisingly enough, their share of endowment funds seems to be disproportionate.

In 1965-66, Catholic institutions of higher education got 38

TABLE 24 Estimated student financial-aid funds disbursed by Catholic institutions of higher education by type of program, type of aid, and academic level of recipient, fiscal year 1965-66 (dollars in thousands)				
		Type of program		
			Federally sponsor	
Type of student financial aid and academic level of recipient		*Nonfederally sponsored*	*U.S. Office of Education*	
			Nonfederal matching funds	*Fede[ral] fund[s]*
Work assignments:				
Undergraduate		$ 7,129	$ 289	$ 2,63
First-professional		166		
Graduate		1,712	4	3
Total work assignments		9,007	293	2,66
Grants:				
Undergraduate		27,810	3	31
First-professional		1,731		
Graduate		4,407		28
Total grants		33,948	3	59
Loans:				
Undergraduate		917	1,953	17,68
First-professional		164	115	99
Graduate		45	158	1,39
Total loans		1,126	2,226	20,04
TOTAL		44,081	2,522	23,30
Percent distribution, all Catholic		59%	3%	3
Percent distribution, total United States		56	3	2
Percent distribution, total United States private		59	3	2

SOURCE: Carnegie Commission on Higher Education tabulation from U.S. Office of Education data.

percent of their student financial-aid funds (Table 24) from the federal government, which is exactly the same as all private institutions of higher education. Another 3 percent came through nonfederal matching funds under federally sponsored programs. The Catholic institutions' use of the funds by work assignments, grants, and loans appears to be similar to that of all private institutions of higher education; the only differences can be attributed to a different distribution of graduates and undergraduates.

It would appear, then, from Table 25, that Catholic higher educational institutions' principal deficiencies in generating income

| Other federal departments and agencies | | Total all funds | Distribution of total, % | | |
nfederal tching nds	Federal funds		All Catholic	Total U.S.	Total U.S. private
37	$ 757	$10,844	15	22	14
	18	186		1	1
	493	2,241	3	8	5
37	1,268	13,271	18	31	20
5	762	28,890	38	25	34
	463	2,197	3	2	3
	1,549	6,238	8	14	15
5	2,774	37,325	49	41	52
34	463	21,055	28	22	22
74	646	1,965	3	2	3
25	227	1,845	2	4	3
133	1,336	24,865	33	28	28
175	5,378	75,461	100	100	100
	7%	100%			
	13	100			
	12	100			

are to be found in the absence of federally financed organized research projects. However, it must be noted that most of the federal research monies go to a handful of elite universities and that the Catholic schools probably do no worse in attracting such funds than other nonelite private schools.

Catholic institutions of higher education disbursed $56.5 million in federal grants (Table 25), 43 percent of which was for organized research. They disbursed $69.9 million in money received from federal loans, mostly for physical facilities (67 percent), the rest going for student-loan funds.

TABLE 25
Estimated
federal funds
disbursed by
Catholic
institutions of
higher
education,
fiscal year
1965 - 66
(dollars in
thousands)

| | Department of HEW | | | |
Funds expended by purpose	USOE	PHS	Other HEW	Departmen of Agricult
Grants and contracts:				
Instruction and departmental research	$ 1,672	$3,915	$863	
Extension and public service	44	10		$17
Organized research	616	9,335	376	13
Other sponsored activities	885	1,589	499	
Libraries	772	2	36	
Student financial aid	3,540	1,941	196	
Physical plant facilities	2,618	85	715	
Other grants and contracts	673	181	97	
Total grants and contracts	10,820	17,058	2,782	30
Loans:				
Student loan funds	20,317	873	443	
Physical facilities	2,275			
Other loans	1,473			
Total loans	24,065	873	443	

SOURCE: Carnegie Commission on Higher Education tabulation based on U.S. Office of Education data.

Current fund expenditures data (Table 26) merely confirm the data reported in Table 24 from a different perspective. Catholic schools spend only about 5 percent of their money on organized research (as compared to 20 percent for all other institutions) and spend relatively more on general administration (15 percent as compared with 10 percent). Catholic schools spend much more on auxiliary enterprises (21 percent as compared with 15 percent), but they also get more revenue from auxiliary services. This is a result of the fact that they are more in the feeding and housing business than the typical American college.

Revenues exceeded expenditures by $19.1 million, or 2.85 percent (Tables 24 and 26), which is good considering that for all private institutions expenditures exceeded revenues. By specific

partment Defense	Department of HUD	Atomic Energy Commission	NASA	NSF	All other	Total expended from federal funds
47		$ 119	$292	$2,199	$307	$9,414
43		98		203	19	434
7,847		1,646	637	2,971	698	24,139
79		1	37	1,640	850	5,580
	$146		6	6	15	983
489		45	278	629	148	7,266
70	2,519	32	6	869	15	6,929
		8		187	646	1,792
8,575	2,665	1,949	1,256	8,704	2,698	56,537
120					110	21,863
	44,234			1		46,510
	25					1,498
120	44,259			1	110	69,871

component, organized research revenues exceeded expenditures by $6.5 million, or 18.6 percent; organized activities relating to education departments revenues exceeded expenditures by $4 million, or 23.7 percent; housing and food services revenues exceeded expenditures by 14.7 percent; and other auxiliary enterprise revenues exceeded expenditures by 8.1 percent. Compared with Catholic institutions of higher education, private schools lost money on organized research, had a smaller return on organized activities relating to educational departments (21.4 percent versus 23.7 percent for Catholic), and had a smaller return on housing and food services (12.8 percent versus 14.7 percent for Catholic).

As a *group,* Catholic higher educational institutions may have

TABLE 26 *Estimated current funds expenditures of Catholic institutions of higher education by function, fiscal year 1965-66*

	Thousands of dollars	Percent distribution			Percent of	
		Catholic	Total U.S.	U.S. private	Total U.S.	U.S. private
Total expenditures	672,353	100	100	100	5	12
Total educational and general	473,362	70	80	77	5	11
Instruction and departmental research	219,448	33	30	26	6	16
Extension and public service	2,642		4	1	1	6
Libraries	24,510	4	3	2	7	17
Physical plant maintenance and operation	59,384	9	7	6	7	17
General administration	103,458	15	10	12	8	16
Organized activities relating to educational department	16,811	2	4	4	3	8
Organized research	35,206	5	20	24	1	3
Other sponsored activities	5,552	1	1	1	3	10
All others	6,351	1	1	1	4	15
Total student-aid grants	37,325	6	3	5	9	14
Total auxiliary enterprises	140,512	21	15	16	7	17
Housing and food services	102,347	15	9	10	9	19
Other	38,165	6	6	6	5	13
Current funds for physical plant assets	21,154	3	2	2	9	17

SOURCE: Carnegie Commission on Higher Education tabulation based on U.S. Office of Education data.

financial problems. But they are in no worse position than other private American higher educational institutions, and may be in a somewhat better one, their current funds revenues exceeding current funds expenditures by 2.9 percent. However, Catholic higher education institutions do not fare equally according to excess of current funds over current expenditures. For colleges with enrollments over 5,000, revenues exceeded expenditures by 1.8 percent; for colleges with 1,000 to 5,000 students, revenues exceeded expenditures by 2.9 percent; for colleges with less than 1,000 students, revenues exceeded expenditures by 4.9 percent; and for the junior colleges for laymen, revenues exceeded expenditures by 8.1 percent. Thus, although we concluded that as a group Catholic higher educational institutions are in a favorable position, the junior colleges and smaller institutions are in a much more favorable position than are the larger colleges and universities.

Insofar as sources of capital funds are concerned (Table 26), the Catholic picture is very similar to all private institutions. Fifty-eight percent of the capital funds come from private gifts and grants. But there is a difference as to which fund receives the money. Catholic institutions are putting their capital funds receipts mostly into physical plants (78 percent) and endowment funds (21 percent), whereas all private institutions of higher education put only about half (54 percent) of their capital funds receipts into physical plant funds, 41 percent into endowment, and 4 percent into annuity and living trust funds. The federal government contributes 9 percent of all capital funds receipts for Catholic institutions of higher education, which is a little better than it does for all private institutions (7 percent). In terms of the total magnitude of this fund, Catholic institutions of higher education account for only 4 percent of the total in the United States, which probably means that they are doing less building, etc., than are all United States institutions.

There is, therefore, in the data in Table 27, some suggestion of a disproportionate Catholic interest in plant expansion and a negative effect on the development of endowment. On the other hand, it may also be argued that because of its past history, the Catholic "system" was sadly deficient in physical plant and is merely in the process of catching up.

Physical plant loans (Table 28) come mostly from the federal government (46 percent) and from private sources (37 percent), which is pretty much the same picture one finds in all private institutions of higher education. Almost all student-loan funds are from the federal government (97 percent). Catholic institutions of higher education account for 8 percent of all physical plant loans and 10 percent of all student loans.

Of particular interest in Table 29 is the section on additions to the plant fixed assets during the year. Catholic institutions did much better than other private institutions of higher education with respect to gifts (7 percent versus 4 percent for all private institutions), mostly of buildings. These data seem to confirm the preoccupation of Catholic schools with expansion of physical plant.

CONCLUSION   While there are some 350 institutions in the Catholic higher educational "system," 21 of these schools with enrollments of over 5,000

TABLE 27
Estimated
capital funds
receipts of
Catholic
institutions of
higher education
by source and
fund, fiscal year
1965 - 66
(dollars in
thousands)

Revenue source	Physical plant funds	Endowment funds	Annui and li trust f
Total capital funds receipts	$79,504	$21,269	$573
Fees charged to students	3,183	183	42
Receipts added to funds from investment of fund	3,621	7,154	184
Private gifts and grants	46,660	11,887	257
Local governments	1,102		
State governments	189		
Federal government	9,328		
Other sources	15,421	2,045	90
Percent distribution of total, Catholic	78%	21%	*
Percent distribution of total, United States	76	21	2%
Percent distribution of total, United States private	54	41	4
Percent of total United States Percent of United States private			

*Less than 0.5 percent.

SOURCE: Carnegie Commission on Higher Education tabulation based on U.S. Office of Education data.

TABLE 28
Estimated
capital funds
loans received
by Catholic
institutions of
higher education
by source and
funds, fiscal
year 1965 - 66
(dollars in
thousands)

Source of funds borrowed during the year	Physical plant funds	Student- loan funds	Tot
Total capital funds borrowed during the year	$126,827	$20,108	$146,
Other funds of the institution	8,335	594	8,
Private sources outside the institution	47,507	6	47,
Local government			
State government	13,274	25	13,
Federal government	57,711	19,483	77,
Catholic, percent of total United States	8%	10%	
Catholic, percent of total private	22	20	

*Less than 0.5 percent.

SOURCE: Carnegie Commission on Higher Education tabulation based on U.S. Office of Education data.

| *ent-* | | Distribution of total, % | | |
s	Total	Catholic	Total U.S.	Private
07	$102,453	100	100	100
82	3,490	3	4	2
38	11,097	11	10	17
49	59,053	58	28	58
	1,102	1	3	
	189		30	1
32	9,560	9	13	7
06	17,962	18	12	15
1%	100%			
1	100			
1	100			
	4			
	10			

| | Distribution of total physical plant funds, % | | | Distribution of total student-loan funds, % | | |
olic	Total U.S.	Total private	Catholic	Total U.S.	Total private
0	100	100	100	100	100
7	5	10	3	3	2
7	43	36	*	1	1
	4				
0	21	15		1	1
6	27	39	97	95	96

	Land	Improve-ment	Buildin
Book value of plant fixed assets at beginning of fiscal year	$143,857	$29,365	$1,703,2
Additions to the plant fixed assets during the year:			
By expenditures	7,492	2,672	137,6
By gift-in-kind from donor	362	53	13,1
By reappraisal of plant value	3,123	104	11,6
By other additions	248	4	6,2
Total additions during the year	11,225	2,833	168,6
Deductions from the plant fixed assets during the year	580	154	10,8
Book value of plant fixed assets at ending of fiscal year	154,502	32,044	1,861,0
Catholic, percent of total United States book value of plant fixed assets at ending of fiscal year	9%	4%	
Catholic, percent of total private book value of plant fixed assets at ending of fiscal year	18	17	

SOURCE: Carnegie Commission on Higher Education tabulation based on U.S. Office of Education data.

have more than 40 percent of all students in Catholic colleges. Catholic schools are concentrated in the Northeast and North Central parts of the country, and generally within the standard metropolitan statistical areas. The most important block within the system consists of 28 Jesuit colleges and universities. Lay faculty predominate numerically over clerical faculty, but the clergy still have most of the important upper-level administrative positions. Faculty salaries are about average when compared with the rest of American higher education as, apparently, is faculty course load. The students at the Catholic schools are not greatly different from other Americans in socioeconomic background, though they are less likely to marry in college or immediately after graduation. They are also more likely to be Irish.

The financial problems of the Catholic schools are probably no

ipment	Total	Distribution of total, %			Catholic, % of	
		Catholic	Total U.S.	Total private	Total U.S.	Total private
6,048	$2,162,474				9	22
3,229	171,053	82	91	88	6	17
818	14,401	7	3	4	20	33
2,081	16,959	8	2	2	24	63
626	7,096	3	4	6	5	11
6,754	209,509	100	100	100	7	18
2,814	14,371				10	23
9,988	2,357,612				9	21
7%	9%					
20	21					

more acute than the problems of American private higher educational institutions in general, and, in some respects, are less acute. Catholic schools, in all likelihood because of the contributed services of members of the religious community, are, as a "system," able to operate in the black while the rest of private higher education has been in the red. They are also getting a better rate of return on some of their auxiliary revenues for the higher educational enterprise. Their administrative costs seem perhaps a bit too high, and they are deficient in obtaining revenue from federal research projects, although presumably only a small proportion of the large private non-Catholic universities in the country are obtaining much income from such projects.

Despite the popular myth to the contrary, Catholic schools as a system are no more deficient in endowment funds than is the rest of American private higher education.

4. *Goals and Functions*

One of the major dilemmas of the Catholic higher educational "system" at the present time is that it must claim to be both educational and Catholic, to be seeking the same objectives that the rest of American higher education seeks, and also to be pursuing objectives which are uniquely its own. The dilemma is not insoluble but neither is it easily resolved. To its critics and to its colleagues outside, the Catholic "system" must say—"our educational values are really the same as yours," while to itself and to its parents and to its students, as well as to some of its critics, it must also say—"but there are some things that we do that most of the rest of American higher education does not or cannot do." If one grants that, by and large, American higher education has committed itself to cognitive development at the undergraduate level and scholarly research at the graduate level, the Catholic schools are, in some fashion or the other, pursuing these goals. But the question then arises as to whether it is possible to be uniquely Catholic in the pursuit of these goals without losing some advantage in comparison with and in competition with other American higher educational institutions.

The question then of what is uniquely Catholic about Catholic higher education becomes virtually the same as the question of what are the goals, explicit and implicit, of the Catholic higher educational "system." It should be noted, however, that in any attempt to answer these questions, two important facts should be kept in mind: (1) Most institutions have a very hard time being specific about their goals, and (2) once an institution is founded, it is relatively easy for it to keep going without any other goals than simply self-maintenance.

Presumably at this stage of American higher education no one takes the statement of purpose at the beginning of college catalogs too seriously. Such writing is a literary genre all its own. None-theless, the rhetoric of the "statement of purpose" can be fallen back upon in time of question and crisis and also may indicate in some vague fashion the problems and dilemmas that a given college faces.

Some Catholic schools are avowedly supernaturalist in their statement of purpose.[1] Thus, one Western college describes as its purpose:

It is the aim and purpose of Carroll College to assist students in the attain-ment of the highest perfection of intellect and will of which they are ca-pable, in order that their earthly life may be spent in the service of God and man, their eternal life in the blessed and complete happiness of union with God in heaven. As a Catholic college, Carroll conceives education to be a preparation for complete living, both in time and eternity, and in conse-quence the prime objective of the instructional program is not merely to teach students how to make a living, but more essentially to teach them to live a good and full life.

And a college from the Middle West views its goals as having both temporal and eternal dimensions:

St. Mary's College (at Notre Dame) receives the girl as a person with a teachable mind. It matriculates her as a student. She is a student in terms of her willingness to learn to think. Her education is the fulfillment of this desire. Her college trains her for temporal existence. This is of relative importance. It educates her for immortality, for infinity, for the Beatific Vision. This is of ultimate importance. The communication of this educa-tion for immortality is her vocation to the world.

Another Middle Western women's college is somewhat more modest in its "statement of purpose":

The College is devoted to helping each young woman develop herself as a person and as a Christian. They acquire the skills and talents to face the future with assurance.

Yet another liberal arts college for women, this one on the West Coast, sees the Christian perspective as providing both the basis

[1] The Maryland Court decision against aid to the Catholic college was based in some part on a strongly supernaturalist description of the school's purposes. Apparently the court justices decided that statements of purpose were to be taken in all literal seriousness.

for articulate criticism of society and also for a special kind of happiness:

The private, religiously-oriented liberal arts college has the special privilege and possibility of grounding its students' appreciation of the world in an admiration of the world's Creator, and of grounding their criticism of society in an understanding of the divine ordering of human relations. Immaculate Heart College for years has added to the liberal arts tradition and to these privileges its own special character of joyful enthusiasm in response to the challenge to change which daily confronts us.

The difference between the last quotation and the previous ones is significant. The last college does not purport to train people for eternity nor even for complete living in this life, but merely in a special perspective for viewing human relationships.

The statements of purpose at the university level generally stress the humanistic goals of liberal education with special emphasis on the idea that a religious institution gives added dimension to the humanistic perspective. One very famous university describes its purpose thus:

The Catholic college of liberal arts is founded within the Catholic world view of which the central fact is that God became man. Therefore as it moves towards the shaping of the Christian intelligence the Catholic college is a special reference for man, his history, his culture, his total life.

The statement goes on to assert:

The liberal arts faculty desires to give its young men the most human, the most durable, and the most useful education of all. The education that allows and assists the young mind to grow upon the real experience of man, to open up to the world in all its wonderful patterns and dimensions, and to become a focus in Christ.

Exactly what it means "to become a focus in Christ" is not explicated.

Another major Catholic university prefaces its commitment to goals of "Christian humanism" with a citation from a papal encyclical: "As a Jesuit educational institution, Boston University shares with all other Catholic schools the purpose defined by Pope Pius XI in his encyclical on Christian education. 'To cooperate with Divine Grace in forming a true and perfect Christian.'" It then goes on to say:

As an institution of higher learning, Boston College has as its objective the conservation, the extension, and the diffusion of knowledge by means of the schools, colleges, institutions, and resources of the University with the purpose of imparting, in the tradition of Christian humanism, an understanding of the unity of knowledge, an appreciation of our intellectual heritage, a dedication to the advancement of learning, and a sense of personal and social responsibility as all of these are known in the light of reason and Divine Revelation.

Yet another major university includes in its concept of total humanism the goals of American democracy and of the Jesuit Order:

Because it is a Catholic university, Marquette College is dedicated to the pursuit of total truth, human and divine, drawing upon the revelations of the past and the discoveries of reason of the present, to enable man to understand himself in his full complexity and to perfect his intellect and will in terms of the intellectual and moral virtues.

Because it is an American university, Marquette seeks to develop in its members a true sense of what it is to be Americans, so that they may contribute to the life and accomplishments of the free and democratic society of which they are a part.

Because it is operated by the Society of Jesus, Marquette emphasizes the spirit of St. Ignatius throughout all its activities. St. Ignatius, the founder of the Society, aimed at developing individual responsibility and flexibility to meet changing circumstances, while motivated by a deep love of Christ.

Exactly what about the university as a Jesuit school distinguishes it from non-Jesuit Catholic universities is not indicated. The quotation itself indicates one of the problems that many Catholic institutions have in elaborating both a theoretical and operational goal for themselves. It is necessary not only that they be uniquely Catholic, but somehow or other they must be uniquely in the tradition of their own religious community.

Yet another large urban university hedges its notion of the development of the whole man. While it is concerned about "the intellectual, volitional, and aesthetic faculties of the student," it nonetheless is quite careful to describe the school as essentially cognitive. The "curriculum is designed to develop the faculty of clear and critical thinking and correct and forceful expression. It seeks to impart a knowledge of scientific principles and skills, an awareness of historical perspective, an understanding of the contemporary scene, and an intelligent appreciation of religious, philosophical, and moral values."

Finally, De Paul University, abandoning the high-flown rhetoric of developing the "whole man," and concern with "volitional" development and "preparation for eternity," is content to maintain that it passes on the Western cultural heritage, prompts the student to ask ultimate questions, and maintains some sort of environment of Christian community and morality.

The purpose of the College of Liberal Arts and Sciences is to provide the best possible liberal education. This is accomplished in a three-fold manner: (a) by giving the student knowledge and appreciation of the great Hellenic and Judeo-Christian culture that is our heritage, with particular emphasis upon the sacredness and dignity of the human personality; (b) by imparting knowledge that leads the student to the possession of intellectual habits that prompt him to think for himself, to express himself articulately, and to ask continuously the question of wisdom—Why?; and (c) by preparing the student for professional life and by developing in him the capacity for further formal education and for self-education.

It is the further purpose of the college to maintain a community of scholars, that is, its faculty, who extend knowledge by study and research and perpetuate the Christian tradition by contributing to it.

Finally, though the college does not exist for this purpose, like all Catholic communities it creates an environment of Christian morality, a function especially important since the College serves young men and women at an age when formative influences are most active.

Allowing for rhetorical excesses, the quotations cited above illustrate the dilemma not only of Catholic higher education, but of the whole of American Catholicism; how can you be simultaneously Catholic and American?—a dilemma which unfortunately many Catholic observers do not realize is not a unique monopoly of theirs.

Formal statements of purpose aside, most of the Catholic higher educational institutions in this country were founded for exactly the same reason that other higher educational institutions were founded in the early history of the country—the training of the clergy—and in this instance, under the category of clergy one must also include religious communities of women. Far more historical research than presently exists would be necessary before one could give exact proportions. It is nonetheless safe to say that the guiding purpose behind the foundation of most of the colleges for women was to provide academic training for members of the religious communities so that they could receive state education certificates for teaching in Catholic elementary and secondary schools. Many of the Jesuit colleges and universities were not started primarily as seminaries, but rather have their roots in the Jesuit secondary educational system in Europe and became higher educational institutions in the American sense only through a slow and, at times, painful evolutionary process. However, many of the other colleges sponsored by religious orders of men and by Catholic dioceses were, to a considerable extent, intended as training institutions for future priests.

Furthermore, the notion of protecting the faith of the immigrants was certainly at the root of the development of a comprehensive Catholic educational "system" in the United States, and while it may have had somewhat less relevance for the higher educational enterprise than it did for primary and secondary education, it was still of some considerable importance at the college and university level. It must be understood that the state school system in many of the countries from which Catholic immigrants came, particularly in Ireland, was viewed by clergy and the laity alike as an instrument for the proselytization of Catholic children away from their faith. Similarly, the "common school" in the United States in the first half of the nineteenth century was thought of as essentially a nondenominational Protestant school where Protestant versions of history were taught and Protestant translations of the Bible were read. The myth within American Catholicism about the young person who went to a non-Catholic college and "lost his faith" was for many years pervasive and powerful, and both clergy and laity viewed non-Catholic colleges as being quite dangerous for their children. While most of the available data suggest that half the Catholics in the country who went to college did not attend Catholic colleges, and that most of them remained firmly within the Catholic Church despite their experience in a "secular" school, the fear of "loss of faith" remained a very powerful motive for a separate higher educational system until recently, and a decline of this fear may be one of the most serious problems that Catholic higher education will face as it attempts to recruit students in years to come.

However, it would be a mistake to think of Catholic colleges as existing merely to train clergy and defend the faith. There was also a notion, though not clearly articulated, that the colleges would develop articulate and dedicated laymen who would play important leadership roles in the Church and also represent Catholicism with credit and honor in the larger secular society. It was never too clear what the components were of this lay leadership and dedication, and exactly what style of behavior was expected to most adequately represent the Catholic viewpoint to the secular world. In the context of the present crisis of Catholic higher education, it is unfortunate that this idea was not thought through too clearly, because, as we shall note in a later chapter, training of a dedicated and competent lay elite would seem to be a goal of Catholic higher education in years to come, and inarticulateness about how this goal is to be achieved has created considerable doubt in the minds of many Catholics as to whether it is indeed achievable in a separate Catholic educational institution.

These historical goals represent something more than merely the rhetoric of a college catalog. The training of the clergy, the protection of the faith, and the development of a well-informed "Catholic laity" have been powerful operating motivations for Catholic higher education, and, to some extent, continue to be important at the present time. However, there are other functions which may be called latent or implicit which help to explain not only the existence, but the persistence, of the separate Catholic system. The emergence of a comprehensive Catholic education at all levels is but one example, though a highly visible one, of the reaction of American Catholicism to its experience as an immigrant religion in a society which, if it was not actively hostile, did not enthusiastically welcome the advent of the Catholic immigrant groups. The comprehensive immigrant ghetto was not only a protection against the assaults of one's enemies, but it also served as an institutional context in which one could be reasonably certain of who and what he was and still adjust to American society. Social scientists are fond of pointing out how the national parishes in the various ethnic groups served as supportive institutions in the transition from the old world to the new, but the entire comprehensive Catholic ghetto played the same role. There is both theoretical and empirical reason to believe that the separate Catholic educational system actually facilitated the acculturation of the immigrant group into American society. And even at the present time, the Catholic graduates of Catholic colleges (in June of 1961) seem to be more successful in the occupational and educational world than the Catholic graduates of non-Catholic colleges. The role of Catholic higher education facilitating ethnic acculturation has not been carefully explored. Yet in the final analysis this may be the most important contribution the Catholic schools have made both to Catholicism and to the larger American society. Obviously, such a role will be of much less importance in years to come.

Secondly, as part of the comprehensive ghetto, the Catholic colleges and universities have served as Roman Catholicism's "intellectual" centers. This is not to suggest that they contributed very greatly to the development of a uniquely American Catholic style of ideology, for very clearly they did not. Theological or empirical research on the problems of American Catholicism has been almost invisible at Catholic universities until very recently, and there were, as far as I am aware, no scholars from the American Catholic universities as consultants of the Second Vatican Council.[2] As we have already indicated in this Profile, most of the research on Catholic education and even on Catholic higher education, has been carried on not at the Catholic universities but at the University of Chicago. However, insofar as there were intellectual leaders in American Catholicism, they did for the most part come from Catholic colleges and universities and served on the faculties of such institutions; many of the most articulate of the new generation of "liberal" and "intellectual" critics of American Catholicism have been trained within the Catholic colleges and universities, and many of them even at the present time are still faculty members in these schools. Catholic institutions thus provided a pool of occupational opportunities for the children and grandchildren of the immigrants who did seek "intellectual" or "quasi-intellectual" careers and would not have much of an opportunity to find them outside of the Church. Furthermore, Catholic higher educational institutions, along with certain magazines, newspapers, and publishing houses, have created an extremely effective communications network in which new ideas, or at least new fads and fashions, can be transmitted with some rapidity to the lay and clerical elite groups within the American Church. This communications network was responsible for the swift diffusion of the theological changes of the Vatican Council to key groups within American Catholicism and continues to play an important role in the modification of the American Church in the postconciliar era. This is not to argue that Catholic colleges exist explicitly or intentionally as part of a com-

[2] Interestingly enough, some European scholars of considerably less competence, particularly in the social sciences, did assist their hierarchies of the Council.

munications network—the function is almost entirely a latent one—but it is reinforced by the "cult of personality" which American Catholics share with their non-Catholic confreres. Each new intellectual or theological hero who appears on the scene is assured that his ideas will be spread rapidly through the communications network, particularly the college lecture circuit.[3]

Finally, the higher educational "system" as part of the comprehensive ghetto has provided an occupational structure in which it was possible for many people within the Catholic "pyramid" to achieve mobility and status that would not have been possible in the larger society. Indeed, some of those who worked their way up within the Catholic pyramid were then able to move over to similar positions in other and more prestigious pyramids—thus the path from an editorship of the *Commonweal* to a staff position on the *New York Times* has been trod by a number of Catholic journalists. Similarly, some Catholic university presidents have achieved prominence and influence in the larger society from their role as key people within the Catholic pyramid that they probably would not have achieved had the pyramid not existed. The existence of many separate status pyramids in American society is acknowledged by most observers of social stratification, who also observe that these pyramids, while they may contain some "mobility traps," also are generally functional for the social organization of American society. Whether such a distinctive Catholic mobility pyramid is desirable in an ecumenical age may be debated by many Catholic theorists. However, it is very likely, given the persistence of ethnic and quasi-ethnic influences in American culture, that the mobility pyramid will, in fact, persist, and that the Catholic higher educational institutions will, in fact, provide many Catholic Americans with high-status positions within the pyramid that they would not be able to achieve outside of the Catholic comprehensive ghetto.

It can be said, therefore, that the Catholic higher educational system has in the past served relatively useful functions both manifest and latent for the Catholic Church and for the larger society. The critical question at the present time is, given the change in the social class of American Catholics and the change in the posture of the universal Church, what, if anything, does it mean

---

[3] One such lecturer has facetiously observed in a parody of *The Report from Iron Mountain* that American Catholicism might not be able to afford "renewal" because it would put out of business so many people who are profiting from the "renewal industry."

to be a *Catholic* college now, particularly when there are a number of critics within the Church who suggest that the two ideas represent a contradiction in terms?

What might be called the avant-garde of Catholic institutions attempts to resolve the problem by moving toward the same standards of academic excellence as prevail in American secular institutions (or at least those kinds of excellence which are thought to prevail there). In interviewing Catholic college administrators, one often finds that they already have the model of the non-Catholic institution they would like to be compared with, whether it be a Catholic Macalester or a Catholic Princeton or a Catholic NYU. There is some fear among this avant-garde, and a fear which is reinforced by criticism from both the right and the left, that, in the process of such movement toward a standard of secular excellence, everything that is uniquely and distinctly Catholic about the schools will be lost. At the other end of the continuum are a handful of institutions which, either in principle or in practice, refuse to move away from their past orientations on the grounds that if they do so, they will lose their Catholic distinctiveness. In between the avant-garde and the rear guard is a broad continuum of other institutions that engage in earnest discussion about what their distinctively Catholic characteristic is. To some extent the discussion is merely theoretical. The great leveling force of the accreditation agencies means that, in most respects, the schools are rather little different from non-Catholic colleges, and that the differences of atmosphere and style are bound to be rather thin and frequently extend not much beyond the rhetoric of the college catalogs already quoted. Furthermore, given the demand for higher education, many, if not most, Catholic colleges will continue in business (at least if their financial problems, like the problems of all private higher education, are taken to be some sort of national responsibility), and will also, given their past history, maintain some kind of affiliation with the Roman Catholic Church for the foreseeable future. Nevertheless, men need their goals not merely to rationalize the continuation of an institution, but also to suggest what options the institution should choose within the framework of constraints under which it operates.

Much of the discussion about what is distinctively Catholic seems to center around what sort of obligations have to be imposed upon the school. Obligatory theology and philosophy courses, obligatory religious exercises, certain courses in philosophy and theology which specify conclusions, a certain proportion of faculty and/or student body of practicing Catholics, certain standards of behavior for factuly and students—all of these have been advocated by some Catholic administrators as the last resort of Catholicism within the Catholic institution. The present writer has heard faculty or administrators say that when the annual retreat is abandoned or the compulsory theology course or the philosophy course in natural theology, which proves God's existence, or when divorced people are admitted on the faculty, or when no more than one-fifth of the faculty is Catholic, then the educational institution will be no different than other colleges and universities. Other administrators, more sophisticated, will assert that the mere presence of members of the religious community on the faculty in any administrative position at all is enough to make the institution Catholic, and that there is no concern at all about the religious beliefs or practices of the lay members of the faculty. However some of these administrators who profess to such theories still are capable of losing many promising recruits to the faculty because there is divorce somewhere in the recruit's family background.

One of the most realistic Catholic administrators responded to the question of what was uniquely Catholic about his institution by saying that he felt it was a few basic ideas to which the school was more or less unofficially committed. When asked what these ideas were, he shrugged his shoulders and said, "Oh, well, that there is a God and that Christ was the son of God, and that he founded the Church—that sort of idea." He was then asked whether these ideas had to be embodied in obligatory course work or in some kind of oath of commitment that at least the majority of the faculty members subscribed to. The president in question looked horrified and assured us that, Oh no, he didn't have that in mind at all; he simply meant that those were some of the ideas that he thought that at least a number of the people in the institution ought to be committed to. In the next question, we wanted to know whether he thought that there was any difference in style between his institution, which was Jesuit in sponsorship, and another major Catholic university sponsored by a different religious order. He looked thoughtful, as though this idea had never occurred to him before (and unquestionably it was raised in the Jesuit recreation room every evening), and then conceded that he could not offhand really think of any important differences between his school and the non-Jesuit schools.

In fact, his particular college was not only distinctively Catholic, it was also distinctively Jesuit in its climate and atmosphere, and will probably continue to be such in the foreseeable future, but its distinctiveness came from a combination of factors—the presence of large numbers of priests on the campus, the religious commitment, more or less, of its student body, the history and conditions which shaped some of the courses of study which were offered within it, and the concerns which occupied the minds of faculty, students, and administrators alike. The president was not denying that his school was distinctive, but rather was very wisely refusing to fasten on any particular element as being essential to its distinctiveness, and was rather content to let the historical, social, and religious processes take their normal course without fear that academic improvement and even some secularization of the board of trustees would, in one fashion or another, destroy the Catholicity of the school.

Such a sensible approach is not terribly satisfactory to intellectual purists who want the schools' uniquely Catholic dimension clearly defined. Nor does it provide much consolation to the nervous and troubled administrator who feels that he is caught up in a social and religious process that he does not fully understand and which he is not sure that he likes. The administrator quoted in the previous paragraph was, on the other hand, nothing, if not secure and serene in his expectations. However, there is a broader context in which the present controversy among Catholic administrators on the uniquely Catholic element in the higher education efforts must be judged.

It seems to the present writer that the weakness in much of the discussion is that it is oriented toward the past, not the future, and asks: "What practices from the past must be preserved in the present and into the future in order that higher educational institutions may not lose their Catholic flavor?" It would be far more appropriate to ask: "What insights, if any, does the Catholic religious position offer that would give some hints about the specific emphases that would be most appropriate in Catholic higher education in years to come?" Thus the proper question would not be: "Do we stop becoming Catholic when we give up obligatory retreats?" Instead it would be: "What new programs can be devised and what new goals imagined that would be an appropriately Catholic response to the problems of American higher education at the present time?" If there are no answers to such a question (and the present writer stoutly refuses to believe that there aren any), then quite clearly American Catholic higher education ha nothing unique to offer, and will slowly evolve toward a situatic where it is no different from other small and medium-sized priva American institutions.

Thus, it would seem that the terms of the present controversy an the context in which it occurs are still largely defined by the imm grant past and by the defensive fear of being overwhelmed by threatening Protestant society, or by a pagan higher education. enterprise. The question is still being asked: "What must we c in order that we might stay different?" A far more appropria question would be: "What particular contribution can we mak in the future that others are not likely to make?" In the concludir chapter of this volume we shall return to this question.

In summary, then, the Catholic higher educational "system arose historically as part of the comprehensive ghetto which wa the inevitable response of the Catholic immigrant groups in th early phase of their adjustment in American culture. The schoo trained lay and clerical elite, reassured parents and clergy tha the faith of the young was being protected, provided an "intelle tual" communications network within the Church, and a status an prestige system not available to Catholics outside of the compr hensive ghetto. As the immigrant experience recedes into the pa and the post-Vatican modernization of the Church continues, man of these functions are no longer accepted or relevant, and th question of what is distinctively Catholic about Catholic highe education becomes, at least on the rhetorical level, crucial. N matter how the question is solved, many if not most Cathol colleges and universities are likely to continue (given federal assi tance) and continue in one way or another to be distinctivel Catholic. But the rhetoric about goals and purposes is not unimpo tant, particularly if the question is phrased in such a way as t refer not to what must be preserved out of the past, but to wha contribution, if any, the Catholic religious vision can make in th future to the total American higher educational enterprise.

5. The Results of Catholic Higher Education

Because it is so extremely difficult to control for input variables, social researchers in higher education have yet to be able to develop an effective methodology for measuring the college "impact." Bright young people graduate from Harvard because bright young people go to Harvard; and many bright young people who go to poor colleges still do very well in both the graduate school and occupational world, not because of anything they learned in their school, but because of their own native ability.

In attempting to assess the question of the impact of Catholic colleges on the students, one must face two issues which have been the subject of considerable controversy: (1) Is there a latent strain of anti-intellectualism within the Catholic religion, or at least within its American branch? (2) Do the Catholic schools either selectively recruit people who are more anti-intellectual or at least reinforce the anti-intellectualism that does exist?

As American Catholicism emerged from the Depression and the Second World War, it began to move beyond the walls of its immigrant ghetto into the main arenas of American life. A number of younger Catholics, intellectuals and journalists, became highly critical of most Catholic institutions and in particular critical of the alleged intellectual failures of American Catholicism. Much of the criticism originated in an organization called "The Catholic Commission on Intellectual and Cultural Affairs," presided over by the Reverend William Rooney, of the faculty of the Catholic University of America. Two major volumes appeared under the Commission's auspices—*American Catholics and Intellectual Life.* by Monsignor John Tracy Ellis, and *American Catholic Dilemma,* by Prof. Thomas O'Dea. Ellis surveyed the empirical data to support the case, while O'Dea constructed a theoretical explanation for the phenomenon of anti-intellectualism. However, the studies

Ellis surveyed described a situation existing before 1950, and O'Dea's elaborate theorizing is not a substitute for the much more simple explanation that American Catholics were, until 1950 still very much a nation of immigrants.

When the present writer began his researches on Catholic college graduates at the National Opinion Research Center in 1961 he fully expected to find a lack of interest in the intellectual life and in academic careers which Ellis and O'Dea had reported for previous generations. Indeed, one Catholic school superintendent asked him to "find out why our kids aren't going to graduate school." However, by the early 1960s, American Catholics were as likely to go to graduate school and plan academic careers as anyone else in the population.

The voluminous NORC research on the subject has been generally accepted in non-Catholic academic circles; lack of interest in academia among Catholics seems to have been an immigrant phenomenon, but the evidence is still viewed with grave suspicion by many Catholic liberals, intellectuals, and journalists.

It should be noted that many Catholic researchers have a strong emotional interest in sustaining the theory of anti-intellectualism for American Catholics. Hence, it has become an important prop in their own ideological assault on what they consider to be the remnants of the conservative defensiveness of immigrant Catholicism. Such writers frequently and generally ritualistically cite the famous article from Monsignor John Tracy Ellis on Catholic intellectualism, ignoring the fact that much of Ellis's data antedate the Second World War, and that major changes have happened in Catholic higher education since the Second World War, and even since Ellis wrote his essay. A number of researchers have wrestled with this problem[1] but the most comprehensive and systematic investigation was made at the National Opinion Research Center by the present writer and his colleagues, most particularly, James A. Davis, Joe L. Spaeth, Peter H. Rossi, and Seymour Warkov. The NORC data are based on four different national samples and five waves of interviews with a large sample of 1961 college graduates and represent a sustained and comprehensive investigation of the issue. While the NORC research on the subject has generally been accepted as definitive, there has been some criticism of it by Lenski and Trent, arguing that the June, 1961 sample was de

---

[1] Most notably, Donovan, Trent, and Hassenger.

ficient in representativeness. The readers of this report need not be detained by the technical controversies over population distribution and sampling variations. The NORC staff has consistently held that Lenski and Trent's criticisms indicate a total misunderstanding of the mechanics of probability sampling. They also have pointed out that a replication of the 1961 sample in a 1964 study done in an entirely different sampling frame confirms conclusively the whole controversy in the appropriate literature.[2] In most of this section, then, we will rely on the NORC studies—at the present time the most comprehensive, the most systematic, and best validated body of data available on the graduates of Catholic colleges.

CAREER CHOICES The career choices of the Catholic college graduate are not so very different from the career choices of other Americans who went to college (Greeley, 1963). Catholics are somewhat overrepresented in large business and somewhat underrepresented in primary and secondary education, but there are no differences between the graduates of Catholic colleges and other Americans in their choice of scientific and academic careers or, within the sciences, in their choice of the so-called hard sciences, such as mathematics, physics, and chemistry. Neither are Catholic graduates any less likely to enroll the year after their graduation in full-time graduate work or to plan an eventual doctorate or a career in college teaching or research. Within the broad categories there are some differences: Catholic college graduates are less likely to choose biological sciences and a little bit more likely to choose the humanities; within the social sciences, Catholics are especially interested in political science, perhaps because they also seem predisposed to government service. But the overall picture from the June, 1961 data is that whatever influence the "religious factor" or religious education may have had in years gone by, there is precious little difference

[2] Following is a list of the relevant literature: James A. Davis, *Great Aspirations* (1964); Andrew M. Greeley, *Religion and Career* (1963), "Influence of the 'Religious Factor' on Career Plans" (1963), and "Religion and Academic Career Plans" (1967); R. H. Knapp and H. B. Goodrich, *Origins of American Scientists* (1952); R. H. Knapp and J. J. Greenbaum, *The Young American Scholar: His Collegiate Origins* (1953); Gerhard Lenski, *The Religious Factor* (1960); Thomas O'Dea, *American Catholic Dilemma* (1958); James Trent, *Catholics in College* (1967); and Seymour Warkov and Andrew M. Greeley, "Parochial School Origins and Educational Achievement" (1966).

TABLE 30 *Degree and career plans of 1964 graduates by religion and school background (uppe* *SES, upper API males only)*

Degree and career plans	Non-Catholic graduates	Catholic Graduates Who Attended:			
		Catholic high school and Catholic college	Catholic high school but non-Catholic college	Non-Catholic high school but Catholic college	Non-Cathol high school and non-Catholi college
Those aspiring to "higher degree"*	57%	55%	52%	53%	48%
Those planning academic careers	15	13	8	9	11
N	(3,619)	(255)	(198)	(78)	(217)

*Ph.D. or professional degree.

between Catholics and Protestants or between Catholic schoc Catholics and non-Catholic school Catholics in their career aspira tions, their graduate plans, or their occupational values.

It is carefully noted in *Religion and Career* (Greeley, 1963) tha the mere plans to go to graduate school do not an intellectual make nor does the possession of the Ph.D. a distinguished scholar make But it is also remarked that the absence of Catholics in the rank of academia, carefully documented by previous research, seems t be rapidly coming to an end. It would seem, therefore, that som sort of dramatic change went on in American Catholicism in gen eral, and within American Catholic higher education in particula in the years between the end of World War II and the inauguratio of John Kennedy.

The findings reported in *Religion and Career* were not accepte by all scholars concerned with the question of the influence of th religious factor on career choice and occupational values. Som writers questioned the validity of the NORC sample and othe suggested that, even though Catholics might have great aspira tions for graduate school training and academic careers, suc aspirations would weaken through the years as the anti-intelle tualism of their religion began to take its toll.

Fortunately, there exist in the NORC studies of college grad uates two very rare phenomena in contemporary social science — panel study and a replication. The June, 1961 graduates were fo lowed for the first three years of their postcollege experiences so that it could be determined whether in fact the Catholic graduates were likely to defect from their career aspirations. Furthermore, working with a completely independent sample of the June, 1964 graduates, Michael Schiltz at NORC could find nothing that did not confirm the conclusions of *Religion and Career*. While the interested reader is referred to the Schiltz work, at least one table from it should be noted in passing. It is obvious from Table 30 that with controls for sex and socioeconomic status, kind of high school attended, and academic performance in college, the graduate of Catholic colleges is no less likely than other Americans (and somewhat more likely than other Catholics) to aspire to a higher degree or to plan a career in the academic life.

The fact that the 1964 study replicated the findings of the 1961 study, with a completely different sample, virtually eliminates the possibility that the 1961 findings could be explained away as the result of sampling variation. However, a more serious criticism is the argument that with the passage of time those who had been

TABLE 31
Graduate school status, by religion, of June, 1961, college graduates (only white males from upper half SES backgrounds who grew up in New England or Middle Atlantic cities with a population of over 500,000)*

Graduate school status	Protestants	Catholics from Catholic colleges	Catholics from non-Catholic colleges	Jews
Those still in graduate school (spring, 1964)	45%	46%	44%	60%
Those with M.A.	12	15	11	24
Those expecting Ph.D.	21	20	15	26
Those expecting academic careers	20	19	15	43
Those in arts and sciences graduate programs	20	22	18	30
Those in graduate school who attend full time	58	57	38	55
Those expecting Ph.D. — when it is expected:				
By 1965	38	28	26	26
By 1967	78	79	62	89
Ph.D. topics chosen	65	70	55	68
N	(163)	(510)	(316)	(121)

*Subsample includes all respondents whose original religion was Catholic and one of every six whose original religion was not Catholic.

tabbed as future Catholic scholars would drift away from graduat school. In June of 1964, there was no sign of the massive defectio of 1961 graduates from academic plans (Table 31). While the di ferences between Jews and Gentiles persisted into the third yea of graduate study, there was no discernible difference betwee American Protestants and the graduates of Catholic colleges in th proportion still in graduate school, the proportion attending grac uate school full-time, the proportion with M.A.'s, the proportio expecting a Ph.D., the proportion expecting to finish their doctor studies in 1967, the proportion having chosen a Ph.D. topic, th proportion studying in the arts and sciences, and the proportio expecting academic careers. The mass exodus from academia tha certain writers anticipated clearly had not occurred by June c 1964. Furthermore, it should be emphasized that the data in Tab 30 have built-in controls for sex, socioeconomic status, race, siz of hometown, and region in which the respondent was raised. (Th differences that exist between Catholics from Catholic college and Catholics from other colleges with the latter scoring som what less high on matters of academic commitment, are not s readily explained. Controls for ethnicity, generation, and mor specific SES controls do not eliminate the differences.)

ACADEMIC
PERFORMANCE

But it might be contended that while Catholics are going to graduat school and planning academic careers, they are still not intelle tual enough or Protestant enough to get into the top-quality grac uate schools or at least to do well in these schools. Actually however, one-sixth of the arts and sciences graduate students i each of the Christian analytic groups are in one of the top 1. schools; and there is nothing in Table 32 to indicate that the grac uates of Catholic colleges are underperforming in the context of th great secular universities. They are just as likely to continue in th schools as American Protestants, a little more likely to have an , grade-point average, just as likely to be expecting the Ph.D. an to have it finished in the middle 1960s, and just as likely to hav their thesis topic approved. Neither is there any sign that they hav in the secular graduate school atmosphere been tempted to defe from their faith (though this surely cannot be said of the Catholic in secular graduate schools who did not have Catholic undergrac uate training.)

Not only did the Catholics who graduated from Catholic co leges and universities in June, 1961 show as much interest in grac

Graduate school and religious status	Protestants	Catholics from Catholic colleges	Catholics from non-Catholic colleges	Jews
Those still in graduate school (spring, 1964)	95%	100%	100%	88%
Those with A grade-point average	10	16	17	14
Those planning Ph.D.	97	98	66	100
Those expecting Ph.D. —when it is expected:				
By 1965	59	56	33	24
By 1966	79	96	47	86
Those having thesis topic approved	50	59	22	19
Those still in religion in which they were raised	55	85	52	71
Those still in religion to which they belonged at college graduation	81	98	54	79
N	(40)	(54)	(27)	(21)

*Subsample includes all respondents whose original religion was Catholic and one of every six whose original religion was not Catholic.

uate school, the arts and sciences, and academic careers as did non-Catholic fellow Americans, but also there was no evidence three years later that in their graduate school performance or attitudes there was the slightest deviation from their original intention. It should be emphasized (though one grows weary of reemphasizing it) that graduate school performance is not necessarily the same as academic eminence.

As they look back on their academic experience, what will the graduates of Catholic colleges think of the education they received? At least on the average, they are no more likely to be critical than any other American graduate (Warkov and Greeley, 1966). However, the one important group of Catholic graduates, the high-performing males who plan to go to graduate school and expect academic careers (especially if their undergraduate college was Jesuit) tended to be much more critical of the education they received than were members of a comparable group who did not attend Catholic colleges.

Thus, while the average graduate of a Catholic college was rea
sonably satisfied with his education, the young people from whom
presumably the Catholic colleges are going to have to recruit thei
faculty members in years to come were something less than enchant
ed with the academic experience they had received. Since we are no
able to find any objective measure of school quality that woul
correlate with this criticism (as indeed it was of the very best Cath
olic colleges that the criticism took place), we are led to deduce tha
it is very likely that this criticism among the future academician
was part of the self-critical inferiority-complex phenomenon cur

Future expectations—want very much to:	Catholic graduates of Catholic colleges	Catholic graduates of non-Catholic colleges	Non-Catholic graduate
Write a book	22%	21%	23%
Make an innovation in my field	26	24	25
Have a great deal of authority	28	25	22
Become well known in my field	41	41	30
Publish in a magazine or professional journal	29	29	33
Be a leader in a community organization	36	29	22
Make a theoretical contribution to science	7	6	7
Become well known nationally	7	6	7
Become an authority on a special subject in my field	40	39	41
Be influential in public affairs	21	15	18
Make a contribution to technology	8	12	10
Be elected to public office	11	17	6
Have poems, novels, or short stories published	11	8	9
Produce original paintings, sculpture, etc.	6	7	7
Have a musical composition played or published	1	2	2
Become famous or eminent	8	4	6
Make a significant contribution to literature or the arts	5	5	7
Make at least $20,000 a year	50	48	41

rently so very powerful in the American Church. It might well be that the most intelligent of future Catholic academicians were influenced by dissatisfaction among some of their younger teachers.

The overwhelming evidence reported thus far in this section is that the graduates of Catholic colleges, while they may be somewhat different in their religious commitment from either other Catholics or other Americans, do not differ very much on any other measure of behavior available to us, and that the "religious factor" is not an important predictor of career plans, occupational values, or academic performance. Nor does it seem (Table 33)

Future expectations— want very much to:	Catholic graduates of Catholic colleges	Catholic graduates of non-Catholic colleges	Non-Catholic graduates
Develop a very successful business of my own	18	18	18
Be elected to a high office in a professional organization	11	8	9
Be a good parent	40	42	43
Have plenty of time for leisure activities	51	52	54
Do something which I consider useful	34	35	35
Have a big family	46	31	16
Be helpful to others	32	30	29
Have a close family relationship	26	24	24
Have good, close friends	21	20	21
Have enough money to live well	60	57	58
Be active in community organizations	56	53	53
Attend concerts, plays, and other artistic or cultural events	41	40	39
Have a nice, well-furnished home	62	58	61
Help my children develop as I think they should	44	43	45
Have freedom from pressures to conform in my personal life	28	26	25
Live in a good neighborhood for my children to grow up in	49	42	45
Do something important	39	38	38
Be able to travel	50	49	51

to be much of a predictor of a young person's expectations, three years after college graduation, of what his life is going to be. The graduate of a Catholic college, for example, is just as likely to feel that he is going to write a book, to become important in his field, to publish a magazine article, to make an important contribution to science or technology, to have literary works published, to produce original works of art or music, to become famous or eminent, to be financially and occupationally successful. And he is just as eager to hope to be a good parent, to have time for leisure activities, to enjoy close friendships, to make enough money to enjoy the good life, to have a nice home, to be close to his children, to have freedom in his personal life, to do something important with his life, and to be able to travel. About the only difference between the Catholic college graduate and the other respondents is that he is more likely to expect (and more likely to want very much) a big family.

RELIGION However, graduates of Catholic colleges are much more likely to remain in the Church and to attend church weekly than are Catholics who do not attend Catholic colleges. Of those who said their religion was Catholic, 97 percent of those who had been to Catholic colleges and only 80 percent of those who attended non-Catholic colleges would still describe themselves as Catholic three years after their graduation. Almost half of the defection from the Catholic Church, among those who went to non-Catholic colleges, apparently occurred before college education began (Table 34). And four fifths of the Catholics who did not attend Catholic colleges would describe themselves as Catholics three years after college graduation. Thus, it would not seem that Catholic higher education has been necessary to keep young people in the Church. On the other hand, there does seem to be some relationship between a Catholic

TABLE 34
Religious defection among Catholic graduates (who were "raised Catholics")

"Raised Catholics"	Attended Catholic college	Attended non-Catholic college
Catholics at beginning of college	98%	92%
Catholics now	97	80
Married to Catholics	86	67
Married to Catholics (spouse "raised Catholic")	81	57
Weekly church attendance	92	67

TABLE 35 *Politics and religion for college graduates and their parents*

Politics	Catholic graduates of Catholic colleges		Catholic graduates of non-Catholic colleges		Non-Catholic graduates	
	Respondent	Parents	Respondent	Parents	Respondent	Parents
Conservative Republican	14%	17%	14%	18%	21%	18%
Liberal Republican	13	13	16	12	22	17
Conservative Democrat	15	19	14	15	10	12
Liberal Democrat	29	25	29	25	20	17
Conservative independent	14	14	9	14	11	14
Liberal independent	13	9	15	14	13	13
Other	2	3	2	2	2	3
TOTAL	100	100	100	100	100	100
N	(1,969)		(2,664)		(2,579)	

college education and church attendance, with better than nine-tenths of those who attended Catholic college reporting church attendance as opposed to only two-thirds of those who did not attend Catholic colleges. Furthermore, those in Catholic colleges were 19 percentage points more likely to have married a fellow Catholic than those who had attended non-Catholic colleges.[3] Whether the strong relationship between church attendance and and Catholic college education can be attributed to the college itself or to the previous influence of the families from which the student was predisposed to go to Catholic college is not known.

POLITICS   It has been lamented frequently by liberals, both Catholic and non-Catholic, that American Catholics, even though they may belong to the Democratic party, are not in fact "liberal" Democrats. It has been further lamented that the Catholic colleges have turned the Democratic children of the immigrant working class into conservative Republicans. It is also quite fashionable among some Catholic liberals to tell rather terrifying stories of the "Birchite" conservatism to be found among their students in Catholic colleges and universities. Unfortunately for these lamentations, the data in

[3] Eighty-one percent of the spouses of the Catholic college graduates were raised Catholics as opposed to 57 percent of the spouses of Catholics who did not go to Catholic colleges. In both instances, there is evidence of a fair amount of "marriage conversions" of people marrying Catholics who had graduated from college.

Table 35 provide no support for their continuation. Thus, about 29 percent of Catholics who went to college (no matter what kind of college they went to) still would describe themselves as liberal Democrats, and only 14 percent would describe themselves as conservative Republicans. If anything, college education seems to make it more likely for a young person to be a liberal Democrat than his parents were. The graduate of a Catholic college is more likely to describe himself as a Democrat, and as likely to describe himself as a liberal, than the non-Catholic who went to college. Attending a Catholic college does not make someone from a conservative family liberal; neither does it make someone from a Democratic family Republican. It can only be said that the tendency of young people to inherit political affiliation and orientations of their parents seems remarkably unaffected by the kind of college they attend.

SOCIAL AND RELIGIOUS CONSEQUENCES

We pointed out previously that the graduate of a Catholic college was more likely to stay in his church and attend mass every Sunday than Catholics who had not gone to Catholic college. At least some Catholic educators, as well as some critics of Catholic higher education, would demand far more than this from a higher educational system affiliated with the Church. Without attempting to enter into the difficult question of how much religious and ethical formation can be expected of a higher educational institution, we can refer to another body of NORC data which gives some idea of the social and religious consequences in adult life of having gone to a Catholic college.

TABLE 36
Religious behavior of college graduates, by kind of college attended

Religious behavior	Catholic college	Non-Catholic college
High on sacramental index	49%	24%
High on Church-as-teacher index	44	34
High on ethical-orthodoxy index	44	33*
High on doctrinal orthodoxy	56	26*
High on religious-knowledge index	65	26*
Children in Catholic schools	73	69
Mass more often than weekly	20	7*
N	(117)	(250)

*Significantly different from Catholic.

TABLE 37
*Social and
cultural attitudes
and behavior of
college
graduates, by
kind of college
attended*

Social and cultural attitudes	Catholic college	Non-Catholic college
High on community-involvement index	43%	41%
High on racism index	19	20
High on anti-semitism index	16	31*
High on anti-civil liberties index	31	44*
High on "Manichaean" index	13	31*
High on religious-extremism index	18	29*
High on anti-Protestant index	39	42
N	(117)	(250)

*Significantly different from Catholic.

In a previous NORC study (Greeley and Rossi, 1966, p. 167) significant and substantial differences were found between Catholics who had gone to Catholic colleges and Catholics who had gone to other colleges on their reception of the sacraments, acceptance of the Church as teacher, in their ethical and doctrinal attitudes, and in their level of religious knowledge (Table 36). It is worth noting that the very substantial differences recorded in Table 36 are not appreciably affected when controls are introduced for sex, social class, or the religiousness of family background. Furthermore, as Table 37 establishes, Catholics who attended Catholic colleges scored significantly lower on indexes that measure anti-Semitism, anti-civil liberties, religious extremism, and "Manichaeanism." These differences also are not notably affected by an introduction of demographic controls.

CONCLUSION In the overwhelming thrust of the vast amount of NORC research material on the graduates of Catholic colleges, there is almost no confirmation for the theory that the graduates of these colleges are academically or socially inferior to the graduates of any American college, and they suggest very strongly that there has been a notable change in the Catholic population and in the Catholic schools since the collection of the data on which John Tracy Ellis based his famous article. This is not to argue that Catholic colleges and universities are all that good, but simply that they are not so bad as to notably impede the academic growth or notably impair the academic effectiveness of the students who attend them. In view of the size and comprehensiveness of the data, one would be forced to conclude that anyone who argues to the contrary does so for ideological and not empirical reasons. It certainly appears that colleges do have some religious impact on their students, though it is very difficult to filter out the self-selection factor. It also appears that a considerable proportion of the lay and religious elite of American Catholicism are trained in Catholic colleges, though here, once again, a self-selection factor may be at work. The arguments, therefore, against the continuation of a Catholic college "system" do not seem to be overwhelming, but neither do the arguments in favor of such schools, at least from the viewpoint of the sponsoring church organization, seem to be decisive. The rest of American higher education must leave this decision to the sponsoring church. From the educational viewpoint, Catholic schools may not be found among the relatively few institutions widely recognized as distinguished, but the rest of American higher education can legitimately view them as an adequate partner. On balance, they are in some instances worse and in a few instances a little bit better than average.

6. Catholic Alumni, after Seven Years

In June of 1968, NORC, under a contract from the Carnegie Commission on Higher Education, administered a fifth wave of questionnaires to its June, 1961 graduate sample. The purpose of this research was primarily to learn the attitudes of the June, 1961 graduates toward higher education in general and on their own alma mater in particular. The major findings from this survey will be reported in another volume, but in the present chapter we will comment on the data concerning the alumni of Catholic institutions. The principal finding to be reported is that while the Catholic alumni are critical of the failings of the schools they have attended, they are, by and large, more sympathetically disposed toward their college or university than is the typical American college graduate. A secondary finding is that there continues to be no evidence that attendance at a Catholic college or university is either an economic or an academic handicap.

Seven years after graduation, when the graduates of Catholic colleges look back on what they think were the goals of their faculty and administrators, they are far more likely than is the typical American alumnus (Table 38) to think that the goals included the development of inner character, training of a responsible citizen, the production of a well-rounded student, and the affecting of the student by the great historical ideas. They are also somewhat more likely to think that their faculty and administrators tended to try and develop the student with good taste and with objectivity about himself and his beliefs. They were less likely than the typical alumni to think that their faculty and administrators were concerned with preparing them for useful careers, or training them in scholarship, or running the university or college as a center for the dissemination of new ideas. The picture that emerges, then, is a school very much concerned with the traditional "liberal" goals of education,

99

	Absolute or top importance	
Perceived goals of faculties and administrations	*Catholic college alumni*	*All alumni*
Develop the inner character of students so that they can make sound, correct moral choices	85%	37%
Produce a student who is able to perform his citizenship responsibilities effectively	57	35
Make a good consumer of the student—a person who is elevated culturally, has good taste, and can make good consumer choices	22	17
Produce a well-rounded student, that is, one whose physical, social, moral, intellectual, and esthetic potentialities have all been cultivated	68	49
Prepare students specifically for useful careers	38	43
Assist students to develop objectivity about themselves and their beliefs and hence examine those beliefs critically	39	38
Produce a student who, whatever else may be done to him, has had his intellect cultivated to the maximum	39	31
Make sure the student is permanently affected (in mind and spirit) by the great ideas of the great minds of history	39	24
Train students in methods of scholarship and/or scientific research and/or creative endeavor	36	40
Serve as a center for the dissemination of new ideas that will change the society, whether those ideas are in science, literature, the arts, or politics	24	27
Provide the student with skills, attitudes, contacts, and experiences which maximize the likelihood of his occupying a high status in life and a position of leadership in society	30	30

TABLE 38
How the alumni of Catholic colleges perceived the goals of their faculties and administrations

though somewhat less concerned with being in the forefront of scholarship and the training for scholarship, and also less concerned about job preparation.

Putting all these reactions together, however, the graduate of the Catholic college is substantially more likely (Table 39) to be strongly attached to his college than is the typical American alumnus. It might be argued that this is uncritical attachment, based on the fact that the graduates of Catholic colleges were not really aware that there was any alternative form of higher education available to them. However, Table 40 casts grave doubt on such an argument. The graduates of Catholic colleges are as likely as any other alumni to say that their classroom teaching was excellent, and somewhat more likely to say that their contact with the faculty and the caliber of their fellow students was excellent; but they leave no doubt about their awareness that the curriculum, facilities for research (including library), and the knowledge and professional standing of the faculty were something less than that to be found in other institutions. It would therefore seem, perhaps in part because of better contact with the faculty, that strong loyalty of the Catholic graduates to their school exists despite their awareness that the curriculum, the library, and the professional standing of the faculty were something less than excellent.

Again, when presented with a table of possible criticisms of their undergraduate experience, the alumni of Catholic colleges were selective in their judgments (Part A of Table 41). They thought that the rules were too restrictive, and that there was not enough opportunity to be of service to the community, or to understand themselves and society, but they were no more likely than anyone else to deny that there was a sense of community in the school, or to assert that the pressure for grades was too intense. Furthermore

TABLE 39
Emotional attachment to colleges

Emotional attachment	Catholic college alumni	All alumni
Strongly attached	36%	26%

TABLE 40
Evaluation of specific aspects of colleges

Specific aspects of college or university attended	Considered excellent	
	Catholic college alumni	All alumni
Caliber of classroom teaching	17%	17%
Curriculum and course offerings	11	18
Facilities and opportunities for research (including library)	9	24
Caliber of the students	23	20
Knowledge and professional standing of the faculty	22	28
Personal contacts with faculty	20	15

TABLE 41 Criticisms of colleges, and courses alumni wished they had more of		
	"Not true at all"	
	Catholic college alumni	*All alumni*
A. Criticisms		
There was no sense of community or chance for students to participate	51%	49%
The rules were too restrictive	28	56
There was no chance to do anything of service to the community	38	52
There was no opportunity to understand society or myself	56	64
It was not intellectually stimulating	58	59
The pressure for grades was too intense	34	35
B. Courses alumni wished they had more of		
Fine arts	60%	53%
Humanities	47	52
Social sciences	56	48
Physical sciences	36	36

(Part B of Table 41), they were less likely than the typical alumni to feel that they would want more courses in the humanities, but more likely to want courses in the fine arts and the social sciences. It would seem, therefore, that the alumni feel that the life of their college was too much isolated from the world, and that their curriculum was defective in both the social sciences and the fine arts, but if anything, superior in the humanities.

Despite their accurate knowledge of the problems and the weaknesses of their institutions, the graduates of Catholic colleges were still strongly attached to them, and Part A of Table 42 suggests that the reason for this is that they are much more likely to feel that their schools helped them to learn how to make their own decisions, helped them to learn how to get along with others, gave them a broad knowledge of the arts and sciences, helped them to formulate the values and goals of their lives, and prepared them for marriage and family life. On some of these items, the difference between the graduate of the Catholic college and the typical American alumnus is quite striking— 19 percentage points, for example, on the institution's helping to form the values and goals of their life. One presumes that at least some of these items have to do with the religious atmosphere and training in the college, but it would also appear that on the traditional items of "liberal" education, such as "broad knowledge of arts and science," and the ability to make one's own decisions, Catholic alumni are more favorably disposed to their colleges than are typical alumni, while on the other hand, the Catholic alumnus is less likely than the typical one to assert that his college trained him for his present job.

The Catholic graduate is also more likely (Part B of Table 42) to say that religious education is one of the important variables he would keep in mind in seeking a college for his children, and that it would be important for a child to attend the same college as he did (Part C of Table 42). Despite the obvious weaknesses of the Catholic colleges, then, they still have been able to provide their students with something that the students consider valuable and

	Catholic college alumni	All alumni
A. How college actually affected me		
Helped me to learn how to make my own decisions	25%	20%
Trained me for my present job	27	33
Helped me to learn how to get along with others	30	23
Developed my abilities to think and to express myself	43	41
Gave me a broad knowledge of the arts and sciences	40	34
Prepared me to get ahead in the world	18	18
Expanded my tolerance for people and ideas	35	34
Helped me to form valuable and lasting friendships	27	25
Helped me formulate the values and goals of my life	39	20
Helped me learn practical and effective ways of helping people	12	12
Helped prepare me for marriage and family life	19	7
B. Importance of religious education		
Religious education would be important in seeking a college for my children	68%	42%
C. Importance of child attending same college		
It would be important for my child to attend the same college I did	28%	18%

TABLE 42
Ways college affected alumni, importance of religious education for their children, and importance of child attending same college they did

Religious behavior	Attended Catholic colleges	Attended non-Catholic colleges
Attend church weekly	82%	61%
Still Catholic	96	87

Designated period	Anticipated income	Catholic college alumni	All alumni
Now	Over $11,000	34%	29%
Six years hence	Over $15,000	54	46
At age 45	Over $20,000	58	42

want for their own children. Part of this is the religious atmosphere in education, but part of it also seems to be the alumnus's perception that the goals of "liberal" education are, to some extent at least, achieved in the Catholic institutions.

While it is difficult to say what religious effect there is from attending a Catholic college, because those who are better Catholics are those who are likely to attend them in the first place, it does appear, from Table 43, that the overwhelming majority of those who went to Catholic colleges are still practicing Catholics, and the suggestion made in some Catholic circles that Catholic education would drive young people out of the Church does not seem to be substantiated.

The graduates of Catholic colleges, then, are well-disposed toward their schools and are apparently better Catholics than those Catholics who do not go to Catholic colleges. Nor has the experience of attending a Catholic college hindered them either economically or academically (Table 43 to 45). The Catholic college alumnus is likely to be making more money than the typical alumnus now, and to anticipate more money both 6 years from now and at the age of 45 than does the typical alumnus. Furthermore, he is also more likely to say that he was "very well prepared" both for graduate school and for a job by his experience in the Catholic college. It must be remembered that in previous research it was discovered that the graduates of the Catholic colleges were just as likely to go to high-quality graduate schools as were the graduates from other institutions, and also just as likely to perform well, academically, in these institutions. Therefore, it would appear that there is nothing either in the occupational or academic experience of Catholics after they graduate from Catholic institutions which causes them to think that these institutions have failed to prepare them. On the contrary, they are more likely than other graduates to say that the schools have prepared them very well for job and career, and their relative success in both career and academia would indicate that their evaluation is not completely uninformed.

Nor is the typical Catholic graduate any less likely to have already obtained his Ph.D. or to be associated with a college or university as an occupation. The critics of earlier NORC reports on this subject suggested that, while Catholics might be as likely as anyone else to attend graduate school, they would drop out along the line (perhaps because of their larger families) and fail to obtain the doctorate. It is perhaps time to declare a permanent moratorium on such suggestions.

Perhaps it is also time for some of the Catholic liberal critics of Catholic higher education to declare a moratorium on their suggestion—taken sometimes almost as an article of faith—that the graduates of Catholic colleges are politically or socially conservative. Part A of Table 47 indicates that they are more likely to be liberal Democrats than the typical alumnus, slightly more likely to be sympathetically disposed to college protesters, less likely to think that scientific research is changing the world too fast,

TABLE 45
College as preparation for graduate school and job

Preparation for:	"Very well" prepared	
	Catholic college alumni	All alumni
Graduate school	36%	30%
Job	31	21

TABLE 46
Academic careers

Academic career	Catholic college alumni	All alumni
Ph.D.	4.3%	3.9%
Employed by college or university	10	10

more likely to think that the protests of the Negroes are healthy for America and to accept the conclusion of the Kerner report that the cause of riots is white racism. They are also less likely to think that Negro militancy is dividing America into conflicting camps, and more likely to urge that the federal government should make a special effort to see that members of minority groups receive a college education. While none of these differences exceed 10 percentage points (save for the reactions to the Kerner report), they are all indicative of a somewhat more liberal attitude in the Catholic college alumni group than among typical 1961 graduates.

Furthermore, even though the Catholic alumnus (Part C of Table 47) is less likely to have experimented with drugs or to have par-

TABLE 47
Political and social attitudes of Catholic college alumni and all alumni

Political and social attitudes

A. Political attitudes

Liberal Democratic

B. Social attitudes

The protests of college students are a healthy sign for America

Scientific research is causing the world to change too fast

This country would be better off if there were less protest and dissatisfaction coming from college campuses

Because the experts have so much power in our society, ordinary people don't have much of a say in things

In the long run, current protests of Negroes in the cities will be healthy for America

The main cause of Negro riots in the cities is white racism

Negro militancy is needlessly dividing American society into conflicting camps

The federal government should make a special effort to see that members of minority groups receive a college education

C. Things alumni have done and would approve if their children did them

Experimented with drugs

Participated in an antiwar protest

Participated in a civil rights protest

Worked full time for a service organization such as the Peace Corps, VISTA, or the American Friends Service Committee

Volunteered to help others (a project to tutor underprivileged students, helping in a mental hospital, etc.)

ticipated in antiwar protests, he is more likely to have engaged in volunteer activities and is more sympathetic toward the idea of his children participating in a volunteer organization. The difference on none of these items is so great that the advocates of Catholic colleges would be able to assert categorically that merely from the point of view of social attitudes, Catholic colleges have been a complete success. Nonetheless, the defenders of Catholic higher education could assert that there is some evidence of moderate accomplishment in the area of social attitudes.

Finally (Table 48), the graduates of Catholic schools are just as likely to read fiction, nonfiction, and poetry, as are the typical alumni, although they are a little less likely to go to concerts, art

atholic college lumni			*All alumni*	
23%			17%	
		Agree		
53%			50%	
21			26	
51			51	
40			39	
64			56	
46			35	
62			67	
63			56	
ive	*I would approve*	*I have*	*I would approve*	
6%	1%	3.7%	1%	
6	14	4.9	15	
2	32	9.1	30	
5	82	2.5	73	
	93	42	91	

TABLE 48
Life styles of Catholic college alumni and all alumni

Activities	Do this frequently	
	Catholic college alumni	All alumni
Read (not necessarily finish) a nonfiction book	38%	39%
Read (not necessarily finish) a work of "serious fiction"	27	26
Read poetry	5	5
Listen to classical or serious music	28	32
Go to concerts	4	8
Go to plays	11	13
Go to museums or art galleries	8	11

galleries, or plays, a phenomenon which may very well be closely related to the fact that they are more likely to say that they would take courses in the fine arts if they had it to do over again.

In conclusion, then, the Catholic alumnus realizes that the curriculum, research facilities, and the faculty quality of his school are not the finest. He also laments the absence of emphasis on the fine arts, and shows some of this absence in his own life style. But he is somewhat more liberal, politically and socially, somewhat more successful, economically and academically, still a practicing Catholic, more likely to be loyal to his school, and more likely to be satisfied both with what the institution tried to accomplish and with what, in fact, it did accomplish in his educational experience. The June, 1961 graduates spent their college years during the tremendous upheaval of the Vatican Council, and have lived through their twenties during the even greater upheaval of the postconciliar era in the Church. Despite these tremendous changes, they still seem more satisfied with and more loyal toward their college than does the typical alumnus, despite the fact that they are capable of being very critical of some aspects of their education.

From the data presented in this chapter, a Catholic higher educator might take reasonable encouragement that his former students do not think he did so badly, and apparently have by no means rejected the idea that such an educational experience would be helpful for their own children. One might even go so far as to say that the alumni seem to be more confident of Catholic higher education in the future than do many Catholic educators themselves.

7. Problems of Catholic Higher Education

Not the least among the problems which Catholic higher education faces is the fact that so little is known about it by those who are not Roman Catholics. The comprehensive religious ghetto is so much a part of American society, even today, that many non-Catholic Americans tend to forget that they may very well know much more about the operations of Bantu bureaucracy than they do about the internal relationships and cultures of American Catholicism. From the outside, Catholic higher education often looks, even to the relatively sympathetic observer, like a mammoth but unpredictable monolith; from the inside it looks equally unpredictable but much less monolithic. In addition to its aura of mystery, however, Catholic higher education occasionally suffers from the fact that ignorance is mixed with a thin residue of nativist religious bias which has not yet been purged completely out of the American body politic. Anti-Catholic feeling may no longer be an important cultural phenomenon in the United States, but some of it is still around, even among the most sophistocated intellectuals and liberals.

This mixture of ignorance and prejudice is confounded even further by the fact that many of those who report on Catholic higher education to "the world outside" are either the professional apologists for the system, whom no one takes seriously, or the professional critics of the system, who have their own axes to grind and who are taken far too seriously by outsiders. Newspaper stories on Catholic higher education, for example, are often accepted far more uncritically than would similar stories be if they dealt with other matters. In short, it is extremely difficult to be simultaneously well informed and unbiased about Catholic higher education. Perhaps the best functional substitute, then, is ambivalence.

An example of the kind of errors that creep into even the most sophisticated analysis of Catholic higher education is to be found in the generally very sensitive description of Catholic colleges written by Christopher Jencks and David Riesman in their book *The Academic Revolution* (1967). Jencks and Riesman are sophisticated, sensitive, sympathetic observers. No one in his wildest moments would accuse either of them of being uninformed or biased. Yet there are four statements in one of their chapters which would not have slipped by in an essay on another subject. Thus, they say "historically the Catholic colleges have never gotten many working-class students." Yet in 1961, one-quarter of the graduates of the Catholic colleges were sons or daughters of blue-collar workers who had not themselves attended college and whose income was less than $7,500 a year. They further assert that education departments in the Catholic universities have not contributed "intellectually to the shaping of public school policy nor have they sought to train a cadre of Catholics who would become leaders in the public schools." They go on to say that "in part this has been because Catholic educators believed that the best way to train a teacher was to provide him (or, more often, her) with a good liberal arts education." They do not add that in many cities where there are large Catholic universities with education departments the public educational bureaucracy has consistently rejected any cooperation with the Catholic university or with anything Catholic in its boundaries.

They assert quite gratuitously that in 1955 "the right-wing Law School Dean, Clarence Manion (of Notre Dame) was probably a fairly representative if slightly exaggerated spokesman for Notre Dame and probably for most of Catholic higher education." There is absolutely no evidence to support such an assertion, and my own impression was that Dean Manion was of considerable embarrassment to the Notre Dame faculty and administration. They also assert that "the Merit scholars *did* have enough money to attend Catholic colleges and all met Catholic college admission standards, and yet they *still* did not come to Catholic colleges in large numbers. This suggests that the appeal of Catholic colleges to the most sophisticated, ambitious, and talented Catholic student is limited— though certainly not negligible." Yet in the very same paragraph, Riesman and Jencks state that 42 percent of the Catholic men receiving an NMS award chose Catholic colleges while 48 percent of the women did so. This is probably somewhat higher than the proportion of ordinary Catholics choosing Catholic colleges. So it would seem that the Merit scholarship winners did, in fact, come to Catholic colleges in *large* numbers, because it is difficult to think of percentages of proportions over two-fifths as being *small* numbers.

I hardly intend to engage in "nit picking" with such scholars and good friends as Professors Riesman and Jencks, but the fact that they could, in the midst of a very sensitive discussion of Catholic higher education, make errors such as this suggests, I would think, the nature of the difficulty for the outside observer in understanding what the "system" in Catholic higher education is all about.

To some extent the mystery results from the failure of even the most elementary public relations expertise on the part of Catholic college administrators. There are, for example, probably far more places available on committees, commissions, and boards for the presidents of Catholic colleges than there are people willing to fill them, and the few administrators who are willing to step into the public limelight are very quickly overwhelmed with assignments. But the problem goes beyond that of public relations. It results in great part from the existence of the comprehensive ghetto of which we spoke in an earlier chapter. Not only Catholic higher education, but the whole of American Catholicism is a mystery to many of even the most sophisticated of American non-Catholics, a mystery which is only partially clarified by the tremendous surge of publicity that the Roman Catholic Church has received since the advent of Pope John to the Vatican and John Kennedy to the White House. The present writer is inclined to suspect that this lack of comprehensive understanding is probably going to be a "given" in American environment for a long time to come. No one can realistically be "blamed" for it. However, it does seem appropriate for someone who is a Catholic but not part of Catholic higher education to suggest to his professional colleagues that it would be wise to resist tendencies to generalize about Catholic higher education on the basis of very little experience or of newspaper stories on the front page of the *New York Times* (or in the *Times* magazine).

SPONSORSHIP As we have indicated previously, most Catholic colleges and universities in the country are sponsored or owned outright by dioceses or religious orders. Until recently, therefore, the boards of trustees of such institutions have been rubber stamps either for the president of the college or for the religious superior who, in fact, is the major decision maker for the college.[1]

As we have also indicated, there has been a strong tendency toward partial or total laicization of the boards of trustees in recent years, but the precise meaning of this laicization for individual schools and for the whole system is still not clear. In many instances it is still specified that the president of the college or university must be a member of the religious community, which means that, for all practical purposes, the religious order has a veto power on the choice of president. Furthermore, even though it may not be fair to the lay trustees to say that they are merely fronts for the religious community, nevertheless they are not likely to be chosen on the basis of their hostility to the religious order, and hence will tend to be sympathetic to the order and its problems. Finally, the religious order will presumably continue to provide substantial manpower and perhaps financial resources to many, if not most, of the institutions in question. Thus, while the legal nature of sponsorship has changed, and while the board of trustees will no longer be mere rubber stamps and will increasingly play a role in the making of broad educational policy for the schools, it remains nevertheless true that there will continue to be, for the foreseeable future, some sort of sponsor relationship between the religious order and many, if not most, Catholic higher educational institutions.

There is nothing inherently wrong in such sponsorship, of course, though there are certain problems which are most certain to arise. As the present writer and his colleagues noted in *The Changing Catholic College* (1967):

The religious community can traditionally be expected to emphasize obedience, discipline, loyalty, order, and respect for familiar, diffuse, particularistic, and ascriptive values. The higher educational institution, insofar as it tries to imitate typical American institutions, will be more likely to emphasize initiative, imagination, creativity and specific achievement, and universal values. A man can have all the talents necessary to be an extraordinarily effective college administrator and yet the provincial, as a representative of the religious community, may think that he cannot safely be trusted with power and responsibility. Similarly, from the point of view of the provincial, the person who would be an ideal religious superior might be a very poor academic administrator. In addition, the provincial and the religious community are very likely to have many other works under their

[1] In some instances the role of mother general of a religious community and the college president were combined in the same person.

direction in addition to higher education. High schools, parishes, missions, retreat houses—all of these are the responsibility of the provincial, and he must view the total needs of the religious order as being superior to the needs of any one specific kind of institution, even if it happens to be a university that aspires to greatness.

As a result, the administrators of Catholic colleges are all too frequently chosen by people who do not understand the needs and problems of higher education and who must be concerned about other needs that sometimes seem more pressing than those of a college or university. In addition, community pressures and the multiple responsibilities of his office may often force a religious superior to view with great concern the innovations that a college administrator might attempt. He may be warned that community traditions are being violated or that the school is being given away to the laity or that grave financial risks are being taken that may bankrupt the religious order. Even if the provincial does not take these pressures seriously, the very fact that the members of the order are in a position to bring these pressures to bear may severely inhibit the freedom of university administrators, especially when the financial officer of the school is more the agent of the provincial or the religious superior than he is of the college president. Under such circumstances, it might be that a Catholic college president would be most effective in accelerating the growth of his school if he were able to structure the relationship between the school and the religious community in such fashion as to guarantee the maximum freedom and independence of the school compatible with its being owned by a religious community.

There is, therefore, a built-in strain or tension between the religious community and the school it sponsors which does not, by the way, necessarily have anything to do with the religious commitment the college makes. The strain is not irresistible, and many Catholic higher educational institutions have resolved it rather well. The critical problem, as we have noted in *The Changing Catholic College,* is to modify the relationship between the religious order and the college so that the administrative officers of the college do not have to report to the religious community for the basic operating decisions they make, and so that the boards of trustees who choose these administrative officers need not be responsible to the religious community for the choices they make. The working out in practice of such restructuring relationships encounters many legal and human problems; but some schools have, in fact, developed such relative independence, though they have done so on an informal and hence not necessarily irrevocable basis. The partial or total laicization of the boards of trustees represents an attempt to give some form of official status to this relative independence of the schools in religious orders. How successful laicization will be remains to be seen, but it is not unduly optimistic to expect that it will have considerable success in guaranteeing the relative independence of the school.

A more generalized version of the problem which exists between a Catholic college and the sponsoring religious community is the question of the school's relationship to the whole Catholic Church. Jencks and Riesman illustrate the problem as it is perceived from outside the system:

The academic professional prefers that his colleagues be chosen on the basis of professional accomplishments and that the choice be made by fellow professionals. An institution which refuses to follow these rules is unlikely to attract appreciable numbers of distinguished scholars over the years for they will not regard it as a "real university." Yet we find it very hard to see how an institution which accepts these rules can long remain Catholic in any important sense. Surely any idea of a Catholic college or university implies some deviation from this narrowly professional and secular standard for choosing the membership of the community, some commitment to judging the human and more especially the moral qualifications of those who will teach the young. A secular university escapes this challenge by saying that it cannot pass valid judgments on such matters except in extreme cases. The Catholic institution makes the same statement. However, what is left of the Church's pastoral pretensions?

There are a number of Catholics who would reply that Messrs. Jencks and Riesman misunderstand the nature of the church's "pastoral pretensions" when they assume that it would be necessary for a Catholic college to pass judgment on the personal lives of its faculty members, and indeed, many Catholic colleges do not pass such judgments and still claim that they remain Catholic in an "important sense." We intend to suggest in the final chapter of this Profile how such a claim can consistently be made, but for the present purposes, it suffices to note that Jencks and Riesman have focused on one aspect of the problem of being affiliated with the Catholic Church and still being as free as one would be at any other educational institution (which in many, many instances is not all *that* free).

It is not the present writer's intention to engage in a theoretical argument whether the ideal Catholic college would have more or less freedom than the ideal public or private institution. Ideal colleges do not, in fact, exist. If one is faced with a more concrete question whether, let us say, Immaculate Heart College in Los Angeles or the University of California at Los Angeles have more or less freedom than their sponsoring agencies, one must return an ambiguous answer. Both have their freedoms, both have their constraints, both have their problems, though it ought to be noted that Immaculate Heart College probably has more freedom for educational innovation than does UCLA, and that both institutions have considerable difficulties with California leadership.

But it is possible to suggest certain reasons, both structural and ideological, why satisfactory levels of freedom are able to exist in Catholic higher educational institutions and do, in fact, exist in many of them.

As we have noted before, the Catholic college system is not coordinated at the present time, and no matter how much coordination may occur in the future, there will remain a vast amount of structural pluralism within the "system" as there is within American Catholicism and indeed the whole Catholic Church. The vast diversity of institutional relationships which has characterized Roman Catholicism for centuries provides structural flexibility of the sort that a reading, let us say, of the Canon Law, would not lead one to expect. Furthermore, the style of leadership which has been traditional in the Catholic Church for centuries emphasizes the wisdom of not pushing conflicts or confrontations to their logical conclusions, but rather finding compromises which eliminate the necessity of appeal to the letter of the law. The law, of course, may still be on the books and may present a potential threat to someone who is ignoring it, but in practice the likelihood of the law being imposed is very thin.

To put the matter more concretely, there exists in Rome a Congregation which in theory has the obligation of supervising Catholic higher education all over the world. Until recently the staff of the Congregation was entirely Italian and largely elderly and had only occasional concern and almost no information about the operation of American Catholic higher education; its interventions, such as they were, were likely to be erratic and at times, quixotic. For reasons unknown on this side of the Atlantic, there was a time several years ago that the Congregation became upset over the fact that American Catholic universities were giving honorary degrees to liberal theologians who had powerful influence on the Vatican

Council (whose conclusions were somewhat distasteful to certain curial officials). Hence, the Congregation insisted on its right to approve all the honorary degrees that American Catholic universities granted. Such intervention annoyed and infuriated most American Catholic administrators, who proceeded to ignore the instruction. One could argue that this irksome but concretely rather meaningless intervention would, nonetheless, obstruct the freedom of Catholic higher education because it represented a potential for further systematic intervention. That it did represent such a potential is undeniable, but on the basis of any reading of the history of the performance of the Congregation of Seminaries and Universities (as it was then called), no one in his right mind would have expected such systematic, heavy-handed intervention. At the present time the Congregation with a new name is presided over by a liberal and urbane French cardinal who would not dream of interfering in the doings of Catholic higher education in this country.

It is possible, too, that on the national level the American bishops might conceivably intervene to impose some sort of restriction or regulation on the freedom of Catholic colleges and universities, but no one familiar with the temper of present relatively conservative American hierarchy thinks they are likely to do so, particularly after the continuing bad press that the hierarchy received on the mistakes made in the administration of the one school for which it has direct responsibility, The Catholic University of America. Finally, it would be possible, again in theory, that a local bishop might interject himself into the administration of a Catholic college and inhibit the academic freedom of the administration or staff of the school. Such intervention does occur, though in recent years it has become so infrequent as to be practically nonexistent. In most instances, the interventions were annoying, unpleasant, and harmful, perhaps, to individual faculty members (particularly when they were members of religious communities), but not systematic and quite possibly no worse than what many state colleges and universities must bear from state higher education boards or legislators. Thus, stern letters would be written to college presidents condemning the showing of *La Dolce Vita,* or recommending the transfer of religious too closely involved in racial matters, or criticizing a reading list on which could be found Salinger's *Catcher in the Rye.* In some instances the university administrations give in to such pressure; in other instances the pressure was resisted, generally successfully. If the interventions have declined in recent years, the reason in part is that administrations are now more likely to resist pressure from local chancery offices; even in the past, one suspects that timid administrations were more to blame for troubles than were reactionary diocesan officials.

Thus, the loose and pluralistic organizational structure and the decentralization of control within the Catholic Church creates a good deal of structural flexibility and guarantees considerable amounts of freedom for higher educational institutions on purely pragmatic grounds. In our extensive tour of Catholic higher education, the writer and his colleagues at NORC were assured by many faculty members, Catholic and non-Catholic, that they experienced in fact more freedom in their classroom teaching than they previously had at state colleges. Some emphasized that there was less supervision of their classroom instruction by Catholic schools than there was in state schools. Even some hard-line Catholic liberal critics were willing to concede that in practice, nobody "bothered" them in the Catholic schools, though they suspected the reason was that "they're too dumb to know how."

Furthermore, in 31 Catholic institutions we visited, we were unable to find a single case where the academic freedom of a faculty member of a Catholic college had been violated by the institution, by the diocese, or by the universal Church. It is worth noting that at the present time only two Catholic higher educational institutions, St. John's on Long Island and St. Mary's at Winona, Minnesota, are on the AAUP censorship list; the former for summarily dismissing a large number of its faculty members without due process, and the latter for firing a young faculty member who married a girl from a nearby Catholic coed college in a civil rather than an ecclesiastical ceremony.[2]

It is not the present author's intention to "whitewash" Catholic higher education on the freedom issue. Some Catholic institutions are horrendously narrow, and their control of student life, as we shall note later, is quite paternalistic, though Catholic colleges have no monopoly on paternalism. Similarly, some Catholic admin-

---

[2] The administration at St. Mary's claims that the faculty member was fired not because he married the girl in a civil ceremony, but because of "scandalous" conduct in the school itself in which he used classroom time to defend and explain his action. However, the reasons given by the college for the dismissal varied from time to time, and the AAUP decided that in any event the young professor's classroom conduct, while objectionable, did not merit discharge. St. Mary's was removed from the censure list in 1969.

istrators would not be willing to admit in theory the doctrine of academic freedom urged by the American Association of University Professors. Finally, there is not in many Catholic colleges an atmosphere of calm, detached pursuit of truth, independent of its religious or pragmatic value. One is forced to say, however, that the ideal of the detached pure *savant* judged only on his scholarly qualities is not honored in universal practice, even at the very best secular universities, and that the differences that may exist between Catholic schools and some other schools here in this matter are more frequently differences of degree, rather than of kind.

However, the issue may still be pressed. Granted that in practice freedom for faculty, and to a lesser extent for students and administrators, is possible in Catholic higher education, is there still not always lurking the potential for conflict because of the theoretical commitment to Catholic "truth" that an educational institution affiliated with the Catholic Church must be expected to make? One must reply that the only "truth" about which there would be a problem would be a religious or theological "truth," so that he would expect the difficulty to be most serious in departments of theology. However, two points must be made: First of all, one wonders what the likelihood is of a formal heretic seeking a position or remaining on the staff of a Catholic higher educational institution in order to preach his heresy. It has not occurred thus far, in any event. Second, in the most progressive Catholic colleges, the theology department is viewed as an academic department much like any other, in which it is expected that a professor make a scholarly presentation and not attempt to either indoctrinate his students or to impose on them his own personal theological position. It is therefore possible for men who are actually heretics or schismatics or infidels (or as they are called in the present jargon, "separated brothers"), to hold tenure appointments in Catholic theology departments and provide sympathetic presentations of their heretical, schismatic, and infidel doctrine to Catholic students. Worse than this, indeed, some of these heretics, schismatics, and infidels are ordained religious functionaries of their particular religion, and their presence on Catholic theological faculties is a source of great joy to their faculty colleagues, to their students, and to the public relations staff of the university. Far from being suspect or unwanted, the Protestant minister or the Jewish rabbi, or even the Buddhist monk whom the Catholic college is fortunate enough to persuade to sign a contract is considered an extraordinarily useful commodity.

One can think of only a single set of circumstances in which the Catholic college or university would find itself caught in an extremely awkward position. If one of its clerical or religious faculty members should leave the Church and begin teaching doctrine opposed to core Catholic teaching (for example, denying the existence of God), simultaneously engaging in a bitter attack on the Catholic Church as an institution, the university might find its devotion to academic freedom put to a severe test. Since an incident of this sort has not, at least to the knowledge of the present writer, ever occurred, it is difficult to say how an administration would cope with it, but it is worth noting that some of the more sophisticated Catholic college administrators in the country would argue that this is the only single instance that they could imagine where they would encounter a major *theoretical* problem in maintaining freedom in their institutions.

There does remain the question, however, as to how an institution such as the Catholic Church, which does have a strong theoretical commitment to its own position as a possessor of absolute truth, can tolerate so much structural pluralism and flexibility. It could be contended that if ever efficient administrators should take over in Roman congregations or in national offices, a reign of terror would be instituted. It would be foolish to deny that witch-hunts have taken place in the Catholic Church in the past, although it would be equally foolish to affirm that the Catholic Church has had a monopoly on witch-hunts. It is not the purpose of this Profile to attempt to elaborate a theoretical statement of the Catholic Church's self-image. However, the question must be raised as to whether the apparent conflict between the structural pluralism of Catholic higher education and the theoretical absolutism of the Roman Church may result in part from a misunderstanding of what that theoretical absolutism really is. Even in the post-Tridentine garrison church, probably the most rigid form that Catholicism has taken in its long existence, much of the rigidity was organizational and disciplinary rather than theoretical. Elite Catholic theology does not lay claim to a great number of certainties, and further cheerfully admits that these certainties are capable of reformulation and deeper exploration and understanding. That some Church leaders have transferred these certainties from their relatively limited domain to other areas, as in the classic Galileo case, is undeniable, and that other leaders have used their positions to impose their own personal religious opinions on some of their followers is further undeniable. But there is a strong and quite orthodox religious tradition within Catholicism that condemns such behavior as an unconscionable abuse of power and argues vigorously that a claim to certainty on a limited number of religious documents need not and ought not impede openness on most of the other scholarly questions to which man addresses himself. At the present time this tradition is in the ascendancy everywhere in the Church, and probably will remain dominant for the foreseeable future.

There is a strain in certain personalities who are confident of their basic religious commitments to extend this certainty to a wide variety of other areas. Thus, a graduate dean may very well feel that it is his obligation to ask a potential recruit to the sociology department whether he has read the papal encyclicals. But he asks this question not in terms of official Catholic teaching, but in terms of his own rather narrow (not to say uninformed) interpretation of Catholic doctrine, and the vast majority of graduate school deans would not only not dream of asking such a question, but would feel that the question was an intolerable violation of what they would argue was the authentic Catholic tradition. The impartial observer from the outside might reply that both the offending dean and his critics could appeal to traditional elements within Catholicism, but he would be forced to concede that the critics have most of the weight of present elite Catholic theorizing on their side.

We have spent several pages on the issue of freedom and the Catholic college because it is important to note in this Profile that both in practice and in theory there seems to be no reason why Catholic colleges and universities cannot be as free as any other private American institution, and perhaps somewhat more free than many public institutions. Some schools are relatively unfree and others are relatively more free. The outside observer, therefore, should once again suspend generalizations and be prepared to evaluate each Catholic institution on its own merits rather than dismissing on a priori grounds the possibility that it might be, in fact, a free institution. He should also beware of the temptation to confuse ethnic-group inferiority feelings and administrative incompetence with the theoretical opposition to freedom.

FACULTY In common with most small and medium-sized private institutions with limited budgets, Catholic schools have difficulty recruiting and maintaining the quality faculty that they feel is appropriate for their ambitions. Senior faculty at Catholic colleges tend to be "locals," many of whom have their degrees from Catholic universities, and in some instances, from the school in which they teach. They think of themselves as teachers rather than as researchers and have a great amount of personal loyalty to the school and to the religious order that administers it, though at times this loyalty is mixed with impatience with what is considered to be lack of imagination and vigor on the part of the administrative leadership. While these faculty members may attend professional meetings, their basic orientation is not toward the professional field, but toward the teaching responsibilities at the institution where they work. Some of them feel frustrated because they have not made it into the academic big-time, while others, perhaps with some rationalization, assure themselves that they are happy not to be caught in the "publish or perish rat race." It is of these senior faculty members that the administrators speak most frequently when they argue that their faculty is a teaching faculty and not a research faculty. In some instances this may mean that the faculty is, in fact, skilled at teaching even though it does not do research. However, in other instances it means simply that it is not able to do research, or has long since given up trying.

The junior faculty, however, has been recruited in the better Catholic institutions during the years when many Catholic schools have made a serious attempt to adopt the standards of excellence of other segments of American higher education and to recruit research faculty from the major graduate schools. Some of the less affluent or less prestigious Catholic institutions must be content with graduate students finishing their dissertations or with the less promising products of the great graduate departments. Other Catholic institutions may be able to recruit very promising young faculty members, but have a difficult time holding them after their academic careers develop, a fact which troubles many Catholic administrators who feel, somehow or other, that a faculty member who is highly mobile may not be quite as loyal as the administrator thinks he ought to be. Finally, some of the best of the Catholic schools are able to recruit and hold moderately distinguished faculty members, and even on occasion, quite distinguished senior faculty who are retiring from major universities. The University of Notre Dame, in addition, has been able to hire men like Samuel Shapiro and James Silver, who were driven out of public schools because of their controversial political stance.

Thus, the junior faculty of Catholic institutions tends to be of far superior quality than the senior faculty, and to receive better pay for its efforts; but it is neither among the very distinguished

younger American academicians nor is it in any sense committe
to a permanent position in the school in which it is employed, an
this despite the fact that once one is "caught" in the Catholic sys
tem, it is relatively hard to break out of it. The doctorate-grantin
Catholic institutions which, as we have noted earlier, enroll a hig
proportion of all the students attending Catholic colleges, have bee
forced to expand their doctoral programs to recruit and hold th
kinds of faculty members which are taken to be the sign of academ
ic excellence in American higher education. While many of the ir
stitutions really are not equipped to go into major graduate pro
grams, they argue that they have little choice if they are going t
attract high-quality faculty. The dilemma that faces all America
higher education, of having to have research scholars in order t
obtain a reputation even if these research scholars are not particu
larly interested in teaching, is simply repeated perhaps with some
what greater pain in the Catholic schools. Many of the liberal art
colleges and minor "universities" would be much better off if ther
existed in American higher education a breed of respected instruc
tors who did not feel inferior because they do not publish and too
pride in their competency as undergraduate teachers. Most Cathc
lic colleges would be much better equipped to compete for skille
and respected instructors than they would be for research scholars
But if they are to attain a reputation for excellence, which the
all would dearly like to have, they have no choice but to seek th
research scholars and experiment with the graduate programs fc
which, in most instances, they do not have adequate financial re
sources.

Jencks and Riesman neatly summarized the state of graduat
education in the Catholic institution:

Catholic graduate schools of arts and sciences have only developed to sig
nificant size in a few of the leading institutions. No Catholic universit
ranks among the top twenty in Ph.D.'s awarded. Catholic University, Notr
Dame, Fordham, and St. Louis are the only Catholic institutions amon
the top 50 producers of Ph.D.'s. Taken together, Catholic graduate depart
ments turned out less than 3 per cent of all Ph.D.'s during the early 1960'
This is a significant increase over the 1950's, and even more so over earlie
decades. Nevertheless, it still meant that the great majority of Catholi
doctoral candidates were turning to non-Catholic graduate schools, an
that even those prospective scholars who earned BA's in Catholic college
usually went elsewhere for graduate work.

Underdeveloped as they may be, the Catholic graduate schools are grow
ing extremely rapidly. This is happening because graduate programs ar

valuable in attracting able scholars to a faculty. Many Catholic progressives deplore this development, arguing that the Catholic colleges should concentrate on undergraduate education and send their BA's to secular universities for advanced professional training. But we know no Catholic college in a position to build a graduate school which is not doing so. In most cases, Catholic graduate departments' aspirations are virtually indistinguishable from their secular rivals, partly because of the need to compete in a secular world. Less and less lip service is paid to the notion of Catholic biology, Catholic economics, or Catholic history. There are separate Catholic learned societies in some disciplines, such as sociology and psychology, but almost nobody imagines that these are substitutes for the corresponding secular societies. The American Catholic Sociological Society, for example, brings together Catholics and non-Catholics studying one or another aspect of Catholicism or of comparative religion, rather than trying to create a new breed of sociologist who would study the full range of social phenomena from a distinctive Catholic viewpoint. A good many religious attend the meetings of this Society because of their specific institutional concerns, but the more professional sociologists among them also attend the nearly simultaneous meetings of the American Sociological Association. Catholic institutions compose so large a world that they deserve special study, by both Catholics and non-Catholics. But this is not the same thing as the unending search for a special Catholic angle of vision with which to approach the regular academic disciplines — disciplines which have been almost wholly organized and subdivided by secular scholars.

Despite small differences in atmosphere, then, it can be said that the Catholic universities are generally very much like second- and third-level non-Catholic ones at the graduate level. They recruit students and faculty from much the same environment, compete with secular institutions for research funds and foundation support, and judge themselves successful or unsuccessful according to their standing in non-sectarian eyes. Most Catholic graduate programs are now eager to attract non-Catholics, both as students and faculty. Able non-Catholics have traditionally been reluctant to join Catholic faculties, fearing not only a loss in professional prestige and mobility but a loss of academic freedom and of voice in institutional policy. But leading Catholic universities are actively trying to allay these fears, and with considerable success.

The Jencks and Riesman description of the Catholic graduate programs is a fair enough description of the faculties at the best Catholic institutions. They compare more or less favorably with the best faculties at the third-level institutions, and some even at the second-level institutions, but they are not distinguished, and are not likely to become so in the foreseeable future. On the other hand, they are reasonably competent, particularly at the better institutions, and in some instances impressively competent by any standards of American higher education. This represents very notable progress in Catholic universities over the situation of even a decade ago.

The smaller and less successful Catholic institutions, of course, have faculties which, by those standards according to which American academicians judge the professional excellence of their colleagues, run from barely adequate to very poor. Since there exist no standards of excellence in classroom instruction, one is not able to say whether the quality of instruction is bad or good in any Catholic institution—or any other one, for that matter. However, there is no reason to think that it is any worse in Catholic schools than in other American colleges and universities, which, let it be noted, is not necessarily a very high compliment.

In the NORC investigation of Catholic higher education, the researchers found that the morale of the lay faculty was generally rather good because salaries were going up and teaching loads were going down at paces which generally seemed to be acceptable. Though few specific complaints about academic freedom could be found, there was, nonetheless, much complaint about the absence of meaningful faculty participation in decision making in the schools. However, in 1966, when the NORC research was conducted, there seemed to be rather dramatic shifts taking place in this area with consultative faculty bodies appearing at many institutions, though it was not yet clear how much power such bodies would have. It further seemed to us that suspicion and distrust toward the administration was strong in many Catholic institutions, in part because of tensions between lay faculty members and clerical administrators. We are inclined to believe that this tension aggravated the ordinary situation of hostility between faculty and administration that is to be found in most higher educational institutions. On the other hand, at some Catholic schools, particularly those which we thought were "high-growth" schools, faculty confidence in the administration's leadership seemed to be high, and faculty optimism about the future growth of the school strong.

The morale of the religious faculty, however, seemed to be much more precarious. We suggested that there were a number of reasons for this problem of the religious faculty (Greeley, 1967):

1   The religious community is of declining importance in the school. While it still may be the inner core, it no longer controls all administrative offices

all the departmental chairmanships, and no longer can view the school simply as a reflection of itself. While this may be viewed, and quite legitimately, as an improvement for the institution, it also can create serious problems for the self-image of the religious on the faculty, especially the older religious.

2 The religious orders themselves are going through severe internal strains and "identity crises" in the current renewal within the Church. It is no longer clear to everybody exactly what a religious order is or what it ought to be doing. A combination of this transition and the declining importance of the religious faculty of the college has led many religious to ask themselves whether they ought to be in the higher education business at all—a question we heard repeated with great frequency during our survey. One young priest who was the only member of the "new breed" in the religious community of a small liberal arts college commented, "If twenty years at this place makes me as stuffy and narrow-minded as my older colleagues I want to get out now."

3 Many religions, both young and old, are going through a personal identity crisis in which the meaning of their religious vocation in a changing world and changing Church is very much in doubt. This identity crisis seems to be especially difficult for the younger religious and those with professional training in the secular graduate schools. There can be no denying that the strain has been very great for many of these young people, and at least some of them have decided that although they are still Catholics, their religious and priestly vocations seem quite irrelevant in the modern world.

4 Many of the older religious faculty see everything they stood for in Catholic higher education going down the drain; the implication of much of the renewal of the Vatican Council and the modernization of Catholic higher education is that the old forms were a mistake. It is difficult to accept the fact that most of your life has been dedicated to that which is now considered a mistake. A religious faculty member at a major university commented to us somewhat wistfully, "This was really a marvelous place in the days before the war. It was small, most everybody knew everybody else, we had great relationships with the students, everything was warm and friendly, pretty much like a family. Now, all we've got here is a great big faculty for turning out degrees."

5 The younger members of the faculty, on the other hand, see the utter frustrations of trying to do what they take it the Vatican Council wants the Church to do in the face of almost insurmountable opposition from older faculty members who simply refuse to accept the post-Vatican renewal.

6 Those in between—those who are neither new breed nor old breed, but half-breed—see time running out on them. Especially those who were long marked as liberals, though they now feel quite conservative in comparison with their younger confreres, and who felt that the Vatican Council was

the legitimation of all they stood for, now wonder if the implementation of the Council is going to reach the grass roots while they are still alive. These members of the half-breed who have had their hopes frustrated so many times before are in many instances not prepared to see it happen once again. Indeed, they are often the most articulate of the critics and the most vigorous of the rebels against what they take to be the establishment within their religious order.

7   Many of the faculty of all ages are dissatisfied with their involvement in what they take to be pastoral work—that is to say, counseling and other priestly or religious activities with young people. To the younger faculty members with their high professional standards, pastoral work with the students is a major dilemma. They enjoy it very much but are afraid that it interferes with their vocation of scholarship. For older faculty members, this sort of pastoral responsibility is something that they think they do not have the vigor and enthusiasm left to sustain. For yet other priests or religious of whatever age, it has become clear that their main attraction to the priestly life or the religious life was the hope of dealing with people, and their academic and administrative responsibilities deprive them of much opportunity for this sort of contact. One brilliant young priest-scholar said to us, "I want to help the kids who come to see me and I also want to do my research. I find the only way I can do the research is to take the telephone off the hook, but it's pretty hard to live with your conscience when you do something like that."

To summarize, then, the problems that Catholic higher education faces with its faculty: Like all other private institutions of medium quality, Catholic schools have a hard time recruiting and holding the kinds of faculty members who, according to the standards of American higher education, will guarantee the school a reputation of having a high-quality faculty. To facilitate recruitment, many Catholic universities have embarked on broad graduate programs which create a serious financial drain and still do not attract the most distinguished of faculty members. Like most other moderate-quality institutions, the Catholic schools have been unable to devise a system of norms by which the quality of faculty would be judged, in part, by the quality of its undergraduate instruction. However, given the fact that only a very small proportion of Catholic schools can be expected even to make it into the second level of graduate education, the evolution of such norms would be important if for no other reason than the assurance of the morale of faculty members. But lay-faculty morale does not seem to be a very serious problem with the rapid improvement of salary, course loads, and faculty participation in decision making. The religious faculty, on the other hand, was caught in a major identity crisis which created serious morale problems that may constitute a major threat to Catholic higher education in the very near future.

In conclusion, the writer will report an impression summarized by a non-Catholic colleague who visited many Catholic institutions. Speaking of the faculty members of his own discipline, he said, "They are not terribly good, though they may be better than they think they are. But they are at least *decent men,* and it is pleasant to deal with them." A number of faculty members who came to Catholic schools from other institutions repeated versions of this summary. In great part, one supposes that whatever reality corresponds to such observations probably results from the absence of the "publish or perish" pressure, but it nonetheless represents an observation of Catholic higher education which ought not to be completely overlooked.

ADMINISTRA-
TION
In the NORC research survey of 31 Catholic colleges and universities, it was concluded that the most serious operational problem that Catholic schools face is the recruitment of competent and effective top-level administrative personnel. It may be possible that in some well-established, financially secure schools (if such exist in American higher education anymore), the president's role is of negligible importance. However, in institutions which are trying simultaneously to stay alive financially and to "make it" academically, the president has a critical role, if it is only to articulate the goals of the school and to rally the support of the various constituencies outside the school whose cooperation is necessary to achieve the goals.

But in the Catholic colleges, the president's role is even more important. Until very recently neither faculty consultative bodies nor boards of trustees provided any limitation on the power of the president. If, in addition, the president is the superior of the religious community, or at least its local branch on the college campus (as is true with most Jesuit presidents), his power becomes even more substantial. Some Catholic presidents, though in our experience a minority, are mere tools of the general or the provincial of the religious order who makes all the major policy decisions, but others are their own masters, and probably enjoy, if they want to, more potential power than most other American college presidents.

However, not all of them are willing to use it. In the NORC

investigations it was discovered that a considerable number of Catholic presidents did not want the job they had, were looking forward eagerly to being able to put it aside, and had been chosen by their religious community, not because of their administrative competency or academic reputation, but because they were either part of the ruling clique within the order or because they were felt to be "safe" men or women who would not cause undue trouble within the religious community and the local chancery office. It was as though the religious order wanted to impose a limitation on the president's exercise of his power, not by structural constraints, but rather by controlling the kind of personality who would be placed in a position of top responsibility.

The situation described in the previous paragraph was not universal. A number of the schools we visited had excellent presidents who were as dynamic and imaginative and independent as any college president in America. Further, a number of schools (9 of 31) had new presidential appointees the year of our study, and in almost all instances these new men and women represented a departure from past tradition.

Finally, the increased power of the trustees and the faculty, while imposing some constraints on presidential freedom, would also demand, one suspects, more vigorous men and women in the presidential office.

Nevertheless, it seemed to the NORC research team that the level of competency of the Catholic presidents could have been higher than it was. In a number of Catholic institutions there were men and women who were obviously of top administrative caliber who would never seriously be considered for such positions because their political or religious stands were thought to be too radical.[3] Further, the requirement in most institutions that the president be a priest or a nun did limit the pool of available talent. One need not subscribe to the principle that laity are better administrators than the clergy to observe that there may very well not be enough clergy with the competence and inclinations to fill at least some 350 top administrative positions in the Catholic educational "system."[4]

While some of the Catholic presidents are quite professional in

[3] Though by almost any objective standards available to an outsider, these men and women were at most moderates.

[4] The present writer is inclined to agree with David Riesman that on balance, the clerical faculty and administrators in the Catholic schools are of somewhat higher quality than the lay faculty administrators.

their orientation, others are still very much amateurs. They are good, well-meaning men and women, who, because of religious obedience, have been forced into positions for which they have no training or skill or inclination. Some of them grow accustomed to and even begin to enjoy the prerequisites and privileges of power, but most can hardly wait until their term of office is over. They do not have the courage to innovate, the personal security to leave, or, in many instances, even the intelligence to understand what their problems are. It would be too much to say that this kind of presidential leader is typical of Catholic higher education, but there are far more of them in office than is healthy for the "system," and far more than is necessary, given the available talent.

If amateurism at the presidential level is on the decline, it seems to be decreasing somewhat less at other levels in the administrations. At some of the best Catholic schools, the second-level administrators are as good as the president, and many of those presiding over the counseling, development, alumni, financial, and registrars' offices are trained professionals. But at other Catholic institutions, the heads of the various administrative departments frequently have no training at all and are much less qualified than their counterparts would be at non-Catholic colleges of similar size and resource. One of the reasons for this problem is that religious superiors are inclined to believe that a reasonably competent man can do almost anything to which he is assigned, even if he has no training, or that a member of the religious community with which there is nothing else to be done would make an excellent registrar or admissions officer.

The problem of amateurism, we found, was particularly serious in the financial offices. In many colleges there was a myth that the financial officer was a veritable genius who had kept the schools solvent despite tremendous difficulties. However, closer examination disclosed that the financial officer was something less than a genius and that his position of power was based on the fact that other administrators knew nothing about accounting and budgetary procedures and were afraid of them. Under such circumstances, the financial officers in a number of institutions seemed, in our judgment, to have far more power than was healthy for the school. Often their power was not matched either by their financial ability or by their understand of the goals of higher education.

Administrative incompetency is not a problem limited to Catholic higher education. The unique dimension of the problem of Catholic colleges is that the historic tradition which has reserved most of the major administrative positions to members of the religious community has made the professionalization of administrative offices more difficult. The religious order is reluctant to remove older or incompetent administrators, is not able to spare its own people for professional training, and is reluctant to pay the price of hiring competent lay people. On occasion it diverts its own problem personnel into such positions. As Catholic higher education makes the difficult transition from a college which was little more than a religious community involved in higher education to an independent institution living up to professional standards established by the rest of American higher education, it is only slowly able to put aside the residues of past practices. It was our impression that in both the faculty and the top-level administrative positions more progress was being made in this transition than it was at medium- and lower-level administrative posts.

Another problem for administrations in Catholic universities and colleges is what we could refer to as the gemeinschaft atmosphere of a religious community in the gesellschaft structure of higher education. In the religious orders, particularly the male religious orders, and more particularly the Jesuit order, the relationship between superiors and subordinates is frequently on a casual and informal basis, though the superior's power is nonetheless real. First names are used, business is transacted over the breakfast table or in the community room, or even in the washroom. Major decisions can be made during a chance encounter in a corridor or at the icebox late at night. Of course there can be no objection to this procedure inside the religious order, but lay people and many younger religious with professional training resent the extension of this style to the structures of a college or a university. They think that professional respect is more important than being called by one's first name and that the introduction of the priest's spiritual role in his relationships with his lay professional colleagues is decidedly inappropriate.[5]

[5] One lay dean at a Catholic college tells the story of meeting with a president priest and a lay faculty member who had been, in the dean's judgment, seriously remiss in his duties. Before the conversation began, the faculty member asked the president to bless a rosary for his wife. The dean commented, "The president immediately became a parish priest again and I knew the rest of the conversation was going to be a waste of time. The priest intimated that it was impossible for him to seriously reprimand a man whose wife wanted a rosary blessed."

This casual and informal gemeinschaft style is frequently called paternalism by some lay faculty members in Catholic institutions. That paternalism exists at some Catholic schools is hardly arguable, and that the paternalism is identified with the spirit of the religious community is also unquestionably true, but paternalism is not limited to Catholic higher education, and the two most paternalistic schools the NORC staff visited during its tour of Catholic higher education were two non-Catholic schools which had been visited for comparative purposes. At one institution in particular, the president exercised minute control over everything that went on in the institution in a way that would unquestionably have led to a revolt at most comparable Catholic universities. Furthermore, the gemeinschaft style, while probably inappropriate in a larger school, need not be paternalistic, but in many instances could result from the religious training of the priest or nun that makes them want to be liked by their colleagues. Unfortunately, they do not understand that inappropriate behavior is likely to be counterproductive when it comes to being liked.

STUDENTS There are two major problems that Catholic higher education faces with its students. The first problem is the replacement of the traditional compulsory religious life that marked Catholic colleges that, until very recently, was taken for granted on the Catholic campus. The residue of this rigid authoritarianism of the past is desperately clung to by some members of the religious community as being part of their tradition, but on the other hand, it antagonizes the younger Catholic students whose family experiences have prepared them for much more permissive and sophisticated use of authority than they frequently encounter on campuses. The second problem is the difficulty that these schools may face in years to come in finding for themselves an appropriate clientele.

The two problems are not unrelated, of course, because if the tensions that exist between the religious orders and the students in the colleges should persist, it seems possible that the present graduates of Catholic colleges would not be particularly inclined to send their children to the same school. The present writer and his colleagues summarized our impressions of the student situation in *The Changing Catholic College* (1967):

There are several theoretical propositions which we take to underlie the attitude of the religious communities toward the students who attend Catholic colleges. First, it is the role of the college to develop virtue in the student, and virtue is something that can be obtained by a repeated performance of obligatory actions. This is a rather curious notion from the viewpoint of educational psychology as well as from the viewpoint of scholastic philosophy, which considers that virtue is acquired by the repetition of free acts. Compulsory daily Mass is now extremely rare in Catholic higher education (though one rather good college still requires it for a couple of months from its freshmen, not so much because the freshmen need it, or profit from it, but as a last final concession to its own old guard). In years gone by, however, even some of the great institutions brought major pressure, formal and informal, on their students to get them into church every morning and to confession every week, under the pretext that this is the way habits would be developed that would stay with the young people in later life. Unfortunately, there never was any attempt to collect data other than anecdotal to prove that this sort of compulsion was effective, but the crowds of students in chapel each morning was surely reassuring to the clergy who thought that they had responsibility for the souls of the young men entrusted to their care.

Even though compulsory church attendance is now relatively infrequent, the compulsory annual retreat is still common in Catholic higher educational institutions. We were assured by otherwise intelligent and sensitive Jesuit educators that when the obligatory annual retreat was eliminated, the school would stop being a Jesuit institution. Despite this, some eight or nine Jesuit colleges have already eliminated the retreat and still seem to be securely in control of the Jesuit order. One Jesuit president remarked, "St. Ignatius of Loyola would be scandalized to know that his Spiritual Exercises have been made a requirement for graduation." Another Jesuit educator assured us that even though the retreat really didn't build up much in the way of good habits, it forced the young men and women to make at least "one good confession" every year and that this was in itself enough justification for the obligatory retreat. It did not apparently occur to him that if only "one good confession" a year was all the young people would make, there might be something drastically wrong either with American Catholicism or with Jesuit higher education. Nor did it occur to him that this one compulsory confession might be obtained at the price of turning the young people against retreats, against Catholic higher education, and against the Church itself. Finally, it has apparently not occurred to some Catholic educators (or for that matter, students or parents) that to expel a young person because he has not attended a religious service which is not required by the general law of the Church might be an atrocious and intolerable infringement of the student's human freedom.

Similarly, it has been argued that the compulsory theology (and often philosophy) program is imperative if a school is to be truly a Catholic university. It is not enough that excellent theology and philosophy programs be offered, but the students must be compelled to accept the offerings or a school, at least in the judgment of many Catholic educators, is no longer a Catholic school. Even though it is a rare institution that still requires forty-four hours of philosophy and theology, some institutions still require that some twenty to twenty-four hours be spent on philosophy and theology courses. It has not occurred to many Catholic educators that they can legitimately insist that philosophy and theology be part of an academic curriculum in any educational institution which is an heir to the Western cultural tradition. The courses are obligatory in most instances not because they are part of education but because they are part of the religious and spiritual development of the young person. The students bitterly resent both the boredom and the compulsion of such courses. The obligatory retreat and the required theology courses are, in the minds of many Catholic educators, absolutely essential for Catholic higher education, independent of any proof that they accomplish anything, and indeed in the face of massive evidence that they create far more problems than they solve.

The second proposition that seems to be widespread among Catholic educators is that the school acts *in loco parentis,* an assumption that is, of course, shared by many non-Catholic institutions. Leaving aside the question of whether the parental role is a feasible one for any college, we must still ask what kind of a parent a Catholic college thinks it is. As one student put it to our interviewer, "I wouldn't mind if they acted the way my parents do at home. Believe me, my parents don't treat me like this. My parents respect my judgment and trust me. I confide in them. But they don't regulate every minute of my day for me and they haven't for the past ten years. That's why I really think I'm leaving this place right after this semester, because I'm used to ten times as much freedom at home."

It would seem that a good number of those responsible for student life at the Catholic university are not aware of the changes in styles of behavior among young people in the contemporary world. Parents do not snoop into the private lives of their children. They do not closely regulate their activity. They do not lay down rigid and elaborate rules that cover every moment of the day. They do not force their children to be religious. They do not distrust and suspect their children, and they do not refuse to engage in honest and open conversation with them. Parents may and frequently do manipulate their children, but if they do so, it is generally in a way so sophisticated that the child does not realize that he is being manipulated. But the regulation, supervision, and constraints of Catholic colleges (as well as other colleges) are often so obvious, so oppressive, so bizarre, and, from the student's viewpoint, so senseless that for the university to claim that it is acting in the role of a parent is a cruel joke as far as the student is concerned. No parent would ever dare treat a child that way.

One of the most dismal aspects of student life on the Catholic campuses is the religious. The old theory of religious life on campus, based on compulsory church attendance, compulsory annual retreats, and compulsory theology courses, is on the wane. In the improving schools, especially, the old policies are being rapidly abandoned. But, unfortunately, it did not seem to us that much in the way of an exciting and meaningful substitute had been found. Despite the dramatic changes made in Catholic worship by the Vatican Council, the general state of campus liturgy was quite discouraging. No more than ten schools had caught the spirit of the liturgical changes of the Vatican Council and provided a meaningful and exciting worship, particularly adjusted to the needs of young people. In some instances, the dull liturgy was blamed on chancel office restrictions, though we could find no evidence that the university had tried to present a very convincing case to the chancel office that campus liturgy ought to be a place for experimentation. At a good number of schools there were still opportunities for young people to attend Sunday Mass the "old way," that is to say, everything was in mumbled Latin, there was no sermon, and the worshippers could get in and out within twenty minutes.

There was enough evidence in the schools where liturgical experimentation was going on that even in its present state the Roman liturgy can be a very meaningful experience for young people. Unfortunately, the majority of Catholic student personnel directors do not seem to be terribly interested in such liturgical developments, quite possibly because many of them are not terribly enthusiastic about developments in the Church at the Vatican Council. At one justly famous Catholic liberal arts college, long a center of liturgical revival, we were surprised not at the poverty of Catholic worship on the campus but that the great liturgical and religious tradition of the school was not exploited nearly as much as it might be with the students. We discovered that most of the students were completely unaware that the abbey attached to the school was one of the great leaders of renewal and reform in the American Church. Here, surely, there was no opposition to reform, but simply no realization that the school had at hand a highly effective substitute for the compulsory religion of the past.

The most serious weakness of student personnel policy in Catholic colleges and universities was not the inadequate housing, the unchallenging religious life, the minute supervision and regulation, the absence of due process in disciplinary cases, or even the pathetic attempts at development of virtue by compulsion. The most serious failure was rather the failure of these colleges to be that which they claimed to be—Catholic. If Kenneth Keniston is right that the basic problem of contemporary youth is the search for meaning, then the most serious failure of any university is its failure to provide an atmosphere and resources by which young people can work out a meaning not only for the private sphere of their lives, but also for the public sphere, and for the relationship between the private and the public spheres. If Keniston is correct that the retreat into privatism and disengagement is the result of the young person's failure to find any system of meaning, then any Catholic college or university that does not give meaning to the private and public sectors of life is proving false to its whole raison d'etre.

Such a failure is particularly depressing in a time like the present, when the Roman Catholic Church is engaged in one of the most vigorous periods of ferment that it has experienced in the past thousand years. One may agree or disagree with Roman Catholicism as a way of life, but it is hard to deny that at the present time the Roman Church is engaged in an exciting attempt to renovate and renew its interpretation of reality and to make relevant to the contemporary world its traditional wisdom. It would not be difficult for Catholic higher educational institutions to communicate some of this excitement to their students. But with the exception of a few schools and a few people in other schools, no attempt is even being made to communicate it. In their role as meaning-giving institutions, the majority of Catholic colleges and universities are pathetic failures.

In revisiting some of the colleges in the 1966 sample, the present writer noted substantial improvement in the student personnel policies. Counseling services are improving, freedom of the press and freedom to invite speakers is widening, compulsory religious exercises are being eliminated, and priests and religious are being replaced in disciplinary jobs by lay people and hence are much freer to play their more appropriate counseling roles. The most striking change in the two years, however, has been what one might almost call a "liturgical revolution." Campus religious services two years ago were, on the whole, drab and dreary. Now, in many institutions, they are lively, imaginative, and extremely popular with the students. As a matter of fact, a tremendous increase of student interest in experimental liturgies (some of them, it must be conceded, quite at variance with ecclesiastical regulations) is almost strong enough on two or three campuses to earn the much overused label of religious revival. The problems reported in 1966 still persist, of course—the authoritarian paternalism of the past is still present and it is still waning. However, as of 1968 the pace of the waning is accelerating.

Jencks and Riesman (1967) describe in the following quotation the second problem that the Catholic colleges face with their students: the possibility that the social and economic population base on which the comprehensive ghetto has been built may well be shrinking and Catholic colleges, whatever their academic improvement, may not improve enough to maintain the clientele in years to come.

Defining a clientele: class

A class analysis of Catholic higher education, past and future, must begin with two basic sets of facts. First, there are the economic constraints and pressures, which affect all private colleges in their competition with state and municipal ones. Second, there are certain social and intellectual constraints and pressures peculiar to Catholic institutions, which affect their competitive position *vis a vis* private non-sectarian colleges and a few state universities. The first set of forces mainly affects the college choices of children from the Catholic lower and lower-middle classes. The second set affects mainly the choices of the Catholic upper-middle and upper classes.

Historically, the Catholic colleges have never gotten many working-class students. It is true that uneducated Catholics must have been somewhat more likely than uneducated Protestants to seek and obtain education for their children; otherwise the educational differences between the two groups would never have narrowed as much as they have. We suspect, however, that the main source of this difference was the fact that Catholics were more urbanized than Protestants. In any case, uneducated parents have not traditionally sent a substantial proportion of their children to college, even when they could afford to do so. Those working-class Catholic families which did send a child to college were often anti-clerical, anti-Irish, or both, and frequently preferred a "neutral" public institution to the available Catholic ones. Sometimes, it is true, they were under economic pressure to choose a Catholic college, since most big cities had a Catholic but not a public college within commuting distance. Sometimes, however, economic pressures worked the other way, pushing Catholics who would have preferred a church college into cheaper secular ones.

In recent years, these circumstances have altered somewhat. The assimilation of more recent immigrants into the fabric of American life has done a good deal to mute anti-Irish feeling, and probably also anti-clerical feeling. In addition, a larger proportion of lower-income children now complete secondary school and enter college. As a result, the traditionally rural state universities have been opening commuter campuses in the major urban centers of their states. At the same time, instructional costs in all sorts of colleges have risen faster than subsistence costs, and it has therefore become more expensive to commute to most Catholic colleges than to go away to state institutions. This will probably be increasingly true in the future. As tax subsidies for state institutions rise, despite Ronald Reagan and his like, those Catholic colleges which have traditionally recruited substantial numbers of lower-income students will find themselves at more and more of a disadvantage. The problem will be especially acute at those colleges which expand enrollment faster than they can recruit religious faculty, for these colleges will experience an especially rapid escalation in costs as they shift over to salaried lay professors. The problem will also be especially acute at the Catholic commuter colleges, for while these colleges cost less than residential ones, the proportional increase in their costs is correspondingly rapid. While working-class incomes are also rising, few working-class Catholics are likely to want to spend their hard-won wage increases sending their children to an expensive Catholic college rather than a cheap public one. Few Catholic colleges have large scholarship programs. The major burden of educating the lower-income Catholic population is therefore likely to fall increasingly on public institutions.

Toward elite Catholic colleges?

Catholic colleges have recently been enrolling about a fifth of all students in the private sector, and that figure seems steady. The decline in their share of total enrollment has been part of the general decline in the size of the private sector relative to the public one. Catholics seem to be almost as willing as Protestants and Jews to enroll in state and municipal colleges if their social and economic circumstances push them in this direction. Catholic colleges are therefore under great pressure to respond in the same way as other private colleges. Most of them will become—if they are not already—elite institutions for a predominantly upper-middle-class clientele willing to pay extra for the presumed virtues of private instruction and a private college BA. A majority of the originally Protestant colleges have long since succumbed to such pressure. In the process they also became less sectarian and more secular, until today many are hard to distinguish ideologically from their public competitors.

While some Catholic colleges are now eager to move in this same direction, the process is beset with difficulties. Catholic colleges have not traditionally appealed to the children of the Catholic social and intellectual elite. In part this was because they were neither intellectually nor socially exclusive, and nourished a pattern of campus life which sophisticated Catholics found repellent. This might not have been a problem if the Catholic elite had been numerous and sure of its ground, for it might then have attended colleges like Notre Dame and Holy Cross and created fraternity-based sub-cultures at odds with the dominant ethos of the campus, just as happened in the better state universities. But this was not encouraged. Furthermore, whatever their feelings about Catholic colleges per se, members of the Catholic elite knew that a Catholic BA was not the best way to get its children where they hoped to go. These students did not want to live their adult lives in an exclusively Catholic context. Instead, they saw their opportunities in much the same non-sectarian terms that non-Catholics did. They therefore wanted to acquire credentials which would open doors in established secular institutions, and they rightly believed that no BA from a Catholic college had quite the same magic as a BA from a leading non-sectarian private college. Even if there had been a Catholic college which was as good academically as the best non-Catholic ones (and there wasn't), the very fact of being Catholic and therefore presumptively parochial would have been a handicap. (The same would have been true of any college with what Americans regarded as a narrowly defined constituency.)

Today the number of young Catholics in this category is growing. The Catholic colleges, having served as a decompression chamber for those climbing out of the ghetto, have now been deprived of this traditional function by changes in what is left of the ghetto, by public competition, and by changes in the economics of higher education. If they are to survive they must define a new function for themselves, and that function seems clearly to be the education of the sons and daughters of their own alumni. These children have in most respects already escaped the ghetto, and they no longer want or need the protection of a Catholic college against the competition of non-Catholic ideas and individuals. They will only choose a Catholic college if it looks like a safe bet in secular as well as religious terms.

Thus, only the sons and daughters of the upper middle class will be able to afford Catholic higher education (barring some extensive government-funded scholarship program), but it is precisely these classes which will grow more and more sophisticated about the greater prestige attached to a degree from a non-Catholic college. Jencks and Riesman are quite correct in noting that this problem is not solved; that Catholic schools may, by the 1980s, find themselves without a substantial population base. It is difficult to argue with the basic dimensions of the problem as Jencks and Riesman see them. To the mind of the present writer, two questions must be asked:

1 To what extent will the comprehensive ghetto survive until the end of the present century, despite the ecumenical movement and the suburbanization of the Catholic middle class? American Jews who have attained greater socioeconomic success than Catholics still maintain a comprehensive system of their own institutions, although their educational network was never as well developed as the Catholic network. On the other hand, anti-Jewish feeling was, and probably still is, somewhat stronger than anti-Catholic feeling, and there is hence less reason for Catholics to maintain their own separate organizations. But the melting-pot model has not been a particularly helpful one in predicting future developments in American society, and ethnic or religioethnic structures may have much greater durability than present estimates would

indicate, particularly when such estimates are based on almost complete absence of research on the latter stages of ethnic acculturation.

2 The answer to the second question may be more under the control of the Catholic colleges or universities themselves. Is it possible for Catholic higher education to evolve a contribution that is more or less uniquely its own to American higher education which would make it attractive to the Catholics of whatever social class, despite the somewhat higher cost of attending a Catholic college? The present writer believes that it is possible for such a unique contribution to be developed and will turn to this in the final chapter. To say that such a contribution is possible, however, is not to say that it is going to be developed.

INTER-INSTITUTIONAL COOPERATION A very simple answer can be given to the question of whether there is much interinstitutional cooperation among Catholic colleges and universities. The answer is no.

The higher education desk of the National Catholic Educational Association has one full-time professional person, one part-time person, and secretarial assistance. The national office of the Jesuit Educational Association is of about the same size. Several other religious orders also have their own national educational association, though with only a part-time staff. Regional cooperative bodies are rare, though there are one-day regional meetings of the college division of the NCEA. In one section of the country the six Catholic college presidents met for the first time at the invitation of the editor of the local Catholic newspaper, who was then promptly elected the chairman of their organization. It was the first time that some of the presidents had met some of the other ones. In the Archdiocese of Chicago there are, in addition to the 6 colleges and universities, some 20 seminaries and sister formation schools that purport to offer some form of higher education. Cooperation and coordination among these institutions is almost nonexistent.

Some individual schools have cross-registration with other Catholic institutions in the area, though the cross-registration tends to be of a rather simple variety which leads neither institution to give up any of its independence or any of its right to duplicate what its neighbor is already doing. Occasional mergers have taken place, and some institutions are moving toward broad interinstitutional cooperation, but usually with considerable reluctance, and at least on one occasion, with the public firing of a president of a women's college who was opposed to what she thought was assimilation by a much larger men's college nearby.

Many seminaries and sister formation institutions are in the process of affiliating with colleges or universities, and there is much talk about the Catholic colleges moving to the campuses of secular universities, though only one or two such ventures have gotten beyond the remote theoretical stage.[6] The rivalries and resentments among Catholic institutions are legendary. At one school we were told by the sisters, after considerable questioning, that the reason for the lack of cooperation was that the priests of the nearby school had tried to steal their land. When, with righteous anger, we pursued the details of this shady land deal, we discovered that it happened over a century ago. At another location two libraries are almost back to back with one another—one library on the Dewey decimal system and the other on the Library of Congress, and with neither likely to budge.

One can assume that most corporate institutions do not like to cooperate with other corporate institutions for fear that they will lose something of their freedom and identity in the process. Yet most American colleges and universities have learned to cooperate, and interinstitutional arrangements and consortia have become quite fashionable, if only out of sheer necessity. But the necessity, if anything, is stronger in Catholic schools, and yet the cooperation and coordination simply do not seem to exist. As we have noted before, if cooperation is the price of survival, one must realistically be afraid that many Catholic colleges and universities would rather not survive.

To understand the paradox, one must attempt to comprehend something of the ethos of the religious order. Each such group has a spirit and a tradition which reach many centuries back into the past. Its members have been trained to be loyal to the image and spirit of their founder and the traditions of the community, and to make the preservation of the community and loyalty to it highly important values. The community is an important reference group; indeed for many, not only the most important but the only truly relevant reference group. Under such circumstances, it is inevitable that rivalries will come into existence among communities and that one group will strongly feel that its traditions are

---

[6] The Immaculate Heart College in Los Angeles plans in 1970 to join the Claremont College group.

far superior to another group's traditions. Hence, intergroup co-operation, difficult at best, becomes well-nigh impossible, because if one cooperates with members of another group, he risks being disloyal to his own traditions. To give up partial control of the sovereignty of one's college runs against patterns of behavior and loyalty that have been sanctioned for centuries, and much of the socialization process of the religious militates against such a risk.

It need hardly be said that such rivalry, factionalism, distrust, and competition are quite foreign to the basic principles of religious dedication to which all priests and nuns subscribe. As one non-Catholic educational statesman who attempted to facilitate the merger of two Catholic colleges remarked, "Apparently they don't understand the meaning of the biblical quotation about he who loses life shall find it." Be that as it may, the distance from general ideals to institutional practice tends to be a long one under almost any circumstances, and particularly long in Catholic higher education. The desire to "do things our way" or to "go it alone" is a powerful one, and the pluralism and inflexibility of the Catholic ecclesiastical structure referred to earlier in the present chapter facilitates such rugged individualism.

It may well be that the federal government will facilitate interinstitutional cooperation among Catholic colleges by making some of its financial assistance dependent on viable programs of cooperation among small colleges.[7] But short of the powerful big stick of federal government pressure or a concerted drive by the American hierarchy to rationalize Catholic higher education—a drive which is most unlikely—there does not seem to be much reason to believe that interinstitutional cooperation among Catholic schools will grow dramatically in the years immediately ahead. Such a situation is unfortunate and is deplored by almost every observer of the Catholic higher educational scene. But even those who deplore it are not very well disposed toward giving up some of the independence of their own college or university.

FINANCIAL PROBLEMS There are a number of difficult analytical problems that one must face if he is attempting to understand the finances of Catholic higher education. First of all, budgets tend to be obscure and, until

[7] Mundelein College of Chicago and St. John's University in Minnesota are already participating in an interdenominational cooperative system of colleges called the Central States College Association, but they don't have many imitators.

recently, even in some very large institutions, practically nonexistent. The presidents of some major schools will admit that they
don't fully understand the budgetary operation of their college.
In addition to not infrequent financial incompetency, and occasionally deliberate obscurity, the problem of understanding budgets
is complicated by the question of the contributed services of the
members of the religious order and the subsidy which their religious community may or may not or may appear to be giving to the
college. Thus, some budgets will list the salaries of their religious
faculty at the regular salary level for their academic rank and thus
show a net loss in annual budget, which is then compensated for
by the return from the religious order of the religious faculty income that remains after the living expenses of the religious have
been paid. On the other hand, other institutions will show a net

TABLE 49 *Federal academic science support to Catholic higher educational institutions*

Catholic higher educational institutions	1966		1963		% chang 1963 - 66
	$1,000s	%	$1,000s	%	
Junior colleges (open to laymen)	290	*	26	*	†
Number of schools supported	(7)		(1)		+600
Colleges (for members of re- ligious communities)	2	*	10	*	—80
Number of schools supported	(1)		(1)		0
Colleges (under 1,000 total enrollment)	5,441	9	616	2	+ 783
Numbers of schools supported	(72)		(41)		+76
Colleges (1,000 - 5,000 total enrollment)	13,569	22	4,006	13	+239
Number of schools supported	(97)		(71)		+37
Colleges (over 5,000 total enrollment)	42,452	69	27,088	85	+57
Number of schools supported	(21)		(21)		0
TOTAL	61,754	100	31,746	100	+95
Number of schools supported	(198)		(135)		+47
Total United States	2,171,050		1,312,201		+65
Catholic percent of total		2.8		2.4	

*Less than 0.5 percent.
†Over 1,000 percent.
SOURCE: Federal Support to Universities and Colleges, Fiscal Years 1963 - 66, NSF 67 - 14.

TABLE 50 *Federal nonscience support to Catholic higher educational institutions*

Catholic higher educational institutions	1966		1963		% change 1963-66
	$1,000s	%	$1,000s	%	
Junior colleges (for members of religious communities)	20	*			†
Number of schools supported	(5)				†
Junior colleges (open to laymen)	897	2			†
Number of schools supported	(25)				†
Colleges (for members of religious communities)	212	*			†
Number of schools supported	(6)				†
Colleges (under 1,000 total enrollment)	9,126	15	231	6	†
Number of schools supported	(105)		(7)		†
Colleges (1,000-5,000 total enrollment	21,035	34	1,444	36	†
Number of schools supported	(99)		(23)		+330
Colleges (over 5,000 total enrollment)	30,563	49	2,324	58	†
Number of schools supported	(21)		(16)		+31
TOTAL	61,853	100	3,999	100	†
Number of schools supported	(261)		(46)		+467
Total United States	846,459		84,504		+902
Catholic percent of total		7.3		4.7	

*Less than 0.5 percent.
† Over 1,000 percent.
SOURCE: Federal Support to Universities and Colleges, Fiscal Years 1963-66, NSF 67-14.

surplus or a break-even on their budget because they list salaries of their religious personnel at a level necessary to provide for the living expenses of these personnel. Still other schools show a surplus or a break-even because they pay their religious faculty nothing, and the religious community itself provides food and housing for the religious teachers. Thus, some schools may show a net surplus income even though they are being heavily subsidized, and others may show a loss which a different accounting system would show as a break-even or a net surplus.

The problem is further complicated by the fact that many of the larger and better institutions follow the first bookkeeping method

TABLE 51   *Total federal support to Catholic higher educational institutions*

Catholic higher educational institutions	1966 $1,000s	%	1963 $1,000s	%	% change 1963-66
Junior colleges (for members of religious communities)	20	*	▲		†
Number of schools supported	(5)				†
Junior colleges (open to laymen)	1,187	1	26	*	†
Number of schools supported	(25)		(1)		†
Colleges (for members of religious communities)	214	*	10	*	†
Number of schools supported	(7)		(1)		+600
Colleges (under 1,000 total enrollment)	14,567	12	847	3	†
Number of schools supported	(105)		(44)		+139
Colleges (1,000-5,000 total enrollment	34,604	28	5,450	15	+535
Number of schools supported	(100)		(75)		+33
Colleges (over 5,000 total enrollment)	73,015	59	29,412	82	+148
Number of schools supported	(21)		(21)		0
TOTAL	123,607	100	35,745	100	+246
Number of schools supported	(263)		(142)		+85
Total United States	3,017,509		1,396,705		+116
Catholic percent of total		4.1		2.6	

*Less than 0.5 percent.
†Over 1,000 percent.
SOURCE: Federal Support to Universities and Colleges, Fiscal Years 1963-66, NSF 67-14.

while the lesser institutions are likely to follow the second or third method and show a paper surplus. But in fact, the position of schools which use the first budgetary method is probably more secure than most of those using the second or third method.

In other words, one cannot assay an analysis of the financial condition of a given Catholic institution without having had precise information about the flow of funds between the institution and its religious community, and this information is not always easy to come by. A mere statement from an administrator that the school is "in the red" or is not "in the red" is largely meaningless until this information is available.

Two other factors complicate even more the picture of finances of Catholic higher education:

1 The financial officer of the school in many cases is quite independent of the academic administration, has longer tenure than the president, frequently feels the obligation to protect the religious community from what he considers the ineptitude of the president, and often has more influence in determining the long-range policy of the school than does the academic administration. Under such circumstances, it is definitely to the advantage of the financial officer to maintain some obscurity about the school's financial situation. While such a condition is not true for the majority of Catholic schools, it is still present frequently enough to complicate further our already confused budgetary picture.

2 In many of the schools, and not excluding the large ones, planning for the future is frequently either nonexistent or very unrealistic, with the result that if overhead expenses of auxiliary activities are not a sign of such activities, then actual expenditures in the years to come are likely to be far in excess of the somewhat whimsical projections that are actually made. The not inconsiderable burden of delayed maintenance, for example, is overlooked in a very large number of institutions.

TABLE 52 *Percent of schools receiving federal support in Catholic higher educational institutions* (dollars in thousands)

Catholic higher educational institutions	Total 1966	Total 1963	Academic science 1966	Academic science 1963	Nonscience 1966	Nonscience 1963	Average total support per school 1966	Average total support per school 1963
Junior colleges (for members of religious communities)	11				5		$ 4	
Junior colleges (open to laymen)	71	3	20	3	71		47	$ 26
Colleges (for members of religious communities)	18	3	3	3	16		31	10
Colleges (under 1,000 total enrollment	97	41	67	38	97	6	139	19
Colleges (1,000-5,000 total enrollment)	98	74	95	70	97	23	346	73
Colleges (over 5,000 total enrollment)	100	100	100	100	100	76	3,477	1,401
TOTAL	75	41	57	39	75	13	470	252

TABLE 53 *Federal support to independent colleges and universities in 1963 and 1966* (dollars in thousands)

Independent colleges and universities	Total			Academic science		
	1963	*1966*	*% increase*	*1963*	*1966*	*% increase*
Under 1,000 total enrollment	4,293	13,822	+222	2,163	5,228	+142
Number of schools supported	(27)	(63)	+133	(27)	(39)	+44
1,000 - 5,000 total enrollment	11,686	27,313	+134	10,847	15,467	+43
Number of schools supported	(55)	(65)	+18	(52)	(63)	+21
5,000 - 10,000 total enrollment	12,342	25,200	+104	11,764	20,236	+72
Number of schools supported	(9)	(11)	+22	(9)	(11)	+22
Over 10,000 total enrollment	314	4,400	*	208	995	+378
Number of schools supported	(3)	(3)	0	(3)	(3)	0
TOTAL	28,635	70,735	147	24,982	41,926	+68
Number of schools supported	(94)	(142)	+51	(91)	(116)	+27
Total United States	1,396,705	3,017,509	+116	1,312,201	2,171,050	+65
Percent of total United States	2%	2%		2%	2%	

*Greater than 999 percent.
SOURCE: National Science Foundation.

Given the existence of these obscuring factors and also given the fact that there has been no systematic study of the finances of Catholic higher education, one generalizes on the subject with considerable hesitancy. Nevertheless, the following general observations can be made with some confidence:

1 Almost all Catholic institutions must live off of tuition and contributions, since, with the exception of one or two schools, endowment is practically nonexistent.

2 The contributed services of the religious faculty which have provided what often is called a "living endowment" for Catholic higher education are bound to decline in the years to come both because of

the decrease in religious vocations and the increased necessity of hiring lay faculty members.

3   The upgrading of lay faculty salary has created a severe financial burden on most Catholic schools, a burden which in almost every case must be met by raising tuition.

4   There is a limit to how much tuition can be raised before enrollment begins to decline. Some of the smaller and less prestigious Catholic institutions are already suffering enrollment decline, though the better schools seem to be maintaining and even increasing their enrollment levels. (Preliminary reports of 1969 enrollment in Catholic colleges indicate an upswing.)

5   Large foundation grants have not always been a benefit to the Catholic schools because these grants move them to a level of financial expenditure that they are unable to maintain when the grants do not continue, and the salary-tuition bind grows severe.

6   Most fund-raising programs at Catholic schools are inadequate both because it would seem that American Catholics are not as generous in contributions as Jews or Protestants and because the fund-raising drives often are inept.[8]

7   The obscurities of the church-state issue in some parts of the country create considerable uncertainties about whether Catholic institutions will receive the government help that they need to survive. In these areas the schools cannot afford to count on such governmental aid.

8   While graduate school programs in the arts and sciences bring considerable prestige to an institution, they also create a heavy

[8] Perhaps it should be observed that there is no rationalized national fund-raising program for American Catholicism. Dioceses, hospitals, churches, local parishes, religious communities, high schools, colleges, universities, old people's homes — all run their separate fund-raising campaigns, only occasionally coordinated by a strong-minded bishop. There is no national fund-raising coordinated by the hierarchy. It may be safe to assume that funds given to Catholic colleges and universities might be given to other charitable organizations if the colleges and universities do not seek the money. However, to the present observer, it seems much more likely that the utter chaos of Catholicism's fund raising means that the aggregate contribution to Catholic institutions is much less than it might have been if there was not so much confusion and competition.

financial drain that is taxing many of the larger Catholic institutions to the absolute limit of their resources.

9 The accompanying tables (Tables 49 through 53) show that Catholic institutions have made an impressive improvement in the
amount of federal funds they have obtained in the years between
1963 and 1966, but there is still considerable room for doubt that
pursuit of such funds is alert or aggressive enough.

10 Many of the Catholic schools which the author visited in preparing the present Profile are operating at a very grim operational
deficit; some of them have been forced to deplete or liquidate their
endowment and others to raise their tuitions to levels which could
easily lead to drastic decline in enrollment and a repetition during
the coming academic year of the financial problems of the previous
year.

11 There seems to be considerable cooperation between Catholic
schools and other private schools to obtain financial help, particularly in the form of scholarship programs from state legislatures.

12 Even schools which are in a relatively strong financial position at
the present time seem to assume that five more years is the most
that they could expect before their financial problems become acute;
the weaker schools need better administration and better fund raising, but even these improvements probably would not carry them
very far beyond 1975.

13 Most of the administrators with whom I talked stressed three kinds
of need: (1) assistance to meet the increased costs of plant maintenance; (2) a vastly expanded program of scholarships which would
enable the Catholic schools to maintain some kind of competitive
market, vis-a-vis the state universities and junior colleges; and
(3) some system of formula aid per student in which the government
(state or federal) would subsidize the school on a per student basis.

In conclusion, it would appear that, like all other private schools,
the financial situation of Catholic higher education is serious; it
may even be more serious in the Catholic schools because of their
dependence on tuition to pay most of their operating expenses and
because the future attractiveness of these schools for the Catholic

population seems to be dubious. It is safe to predict that many of the smaller and weaker Catholic schools may not survive into the 1980s; the larger and better schools probably will, but it will be a perilous adventure.

CONCLUSION At the end of this lengthy list of problems, we are in a position to summarize by saying that most of the structural problems of Catholic colleges and universities come either from the fact that they are sponsored by religious communities or that they are part of the comprehensive ghetto which was the Catholic population's response to the immigrant experience in this country. Both the religious orders and the comprehensive ghetto are undergoing major change, and some of it at an extraordinarily rapid pace. Thus, the partial laicization of boards of trustees and the campus liturgical revival have made dramatic progress in the two years since the NORC team visited its sample of Catholic colleges. Despite the pace of change, the schools have not yet resolved the problem of their relationships with the sponsoring religious communities; nor have they evolved for themselves a satisfactory rationale for their existence as the comprehensive ghetto goes into the final stages of the acculturation process. Faculty quality of the Catholic schools is, on the average, presentable, and lay faculty morale better than might be expected. But there is as yet little meaningful faculty participation in the governance of the institutions, and the morale of the clerical faculty is poor. The best of the administrators are very good indeed, but amateurism is still rampant. A meaningful religious life for the students has not yet replaced the compulsory religiousness of the past or the vacuum created by the elimination of compulsions. Freedom in the broad sense of the word does exist in the Catholic institutions, partly because of structural pluralism and partly because of certain theoretical elements in the Catholic tradition, but narrowness, rigidity, and authoritarian styles also exist, and many faculty members, particularly lay faculty members, are not persuaded that a commitment to academic freedom is much more than skin-deep. The recruitment of students in the future as costs go up and as the Catholic middle class becomes more sophisticated about the status implications of college degrees seems likely to create very serious problems. Cooperation among Catholic institutions is meager but increasing slowly.

The Catholic schools, then, must wrestle simultaneously with several difficult transitions. Religious orders are moving from the post-Tridentine to the post-Vatican age. Higher education is moving from a narrowly ecclesiastical perspective to a broadly secular one. Faculty and administration are moving from amateurism to professionalism. Students are growing more restless, the population base may be eroding, and costs are going up. Vigorous, intelligent, and imaginative leadership is needed, but while the quality of leadership is improving, it has still a long way to go to be adequate to respond to the complexities of the problems facing the Catholic schools. Many of these problems are not uniquely Catholic, but some of them are and unfortunately they have come at a time when the financial crisis makes it even more difficult for the Catholic schools to cope with the problems.

Only a naive optimist would, under such circumstances, predict an untroubled future for the 350 Catholic schools, but they are still a substantial segment of the American higher educational enterprise, and it may be too early to write them off. Whether it is in the interest of the rest of higher American education to do so or not is beyond the concern of this Profile, but, in a concluding chapter, we propose to make some comments about the possible contributions of the Catholic schools to the evolving American higher education enterprise.

8. A Tale of Four Schools

In this chapter we intend to describe in some detail four different Catholic universities. All are located in large cities with heavy Catholic concentration, all are close to great secular universities, all are administered by the Society of Jesus, all have over 5,000 students, three grant at least some Ph.D.'s, and all have at least some professional schools. One would suspect that in 1945 the four institutions were very similar; their differential response to the challenges of the last two decades illustrates the problems and dilemmas that Catholic higher education faces.

HOLDING THE LINE The first school is the smallest of the four. Its tuition of $1,200 is the lowest of the four schools. It has a very limited arts and science graduate program, though its involvement in professional education is extensive. It has been able to maintain a balanced budget through a highly successful evening division, competent fund raising in its local community, extremely effective political power because most of the lawyers in the city governments are graduates of its law school, and through the wise use of the contributed services of the religious faculty.

Faculty salary is reasonably high and the faculty quality is reasonably good, but, because it has avoided expensive Ph.D. programs, the school has been able to limit the number of high-salaried and low income-producing graduate school faculty. Since it has not had to raise its tuition appreciably in recent years, its enrollment remains constant and, indeed, is increasing somewhat. Its student body is largely Catholic and quite docile, even though located in the midst of an area of extreme student unrest. Its top-level leadership is amiable but not brilliant; at the second level there is strife between one group which is essentially conservative, budget-minded, and unimaginative in its planning for the school's future and a second group which is greatly concerned about the improvement in the academic quality and the reputation of the school. At the present time the former group clearly is dominant and the school's future is closely planned and tightly budgeted; wherever expansion programs will occur, they will have to have clear financial rationalization before they will be attempted. The school hopes to be able to meet whatever increased expenses it will face out of even more effective fund-raising campaigns than its present highly successful ones or from some kind of state aid for which it is campaigning, together with other private institutions.

Several years ago the leadership at other more progressive Jesuit institutions, pointing to the school as a prime example of what happens to an institution when it is in the hands of narrow and fiscally concerned administrators, observed that, given its location and potential resources, there was no reason why this school could not have become a very impressive university. At the present time, however, the administrators of this school are delighting in the fact that some of their critics are in very awkward financial situations, while they themselves can face the future with confidence, knowing that neither their expenses nor their tuition will likely go beyond safe limits. They may have remained a backwater of American higher education, but they have survived, they are respected in their community, and they are very likely to continue to survive.

THE BURDEN OF A MEDICAL SCHOOL The second college is the largest of the four. Its tuition, like that of the other two schools to be discussed, is about $1,800 a year. It has an extensive Ph.D. program, but only a handful of presentable departments. It was not rated by the other Catholic universities to be worthy of an invitation to a meeting of American Catholic universities.[1] Its major asset as well as its major problem is a medical school which, at least for the last quarter of a century, has been a considerable financial burden to the institution and has also consumed much of its fund-raising energies and much of the time and concern of its top-level administrators. At the present time there is some hope that in the next few years the medical school and its adjoining medical center will be able to "practically" pay for itself, but this is another way of saying that until now the

[1] By university here is meant those schools which, because of extensive Ph.D. programs, can claim to be something more than undergraduate colleges with professional schools attached.

medical school has been a drain on the university, both directly, in that it has operated at a deficit, and indirectly, in that so much of the university fund raising has been channeled into it. Nonetheless, the university has been able in recent years to maintain a balanced budget, at least in part because of substantial state aid in the form of scholarship assistance to its students. The presence of a large state university near it had led initially to a decline in its enrollment, but the state scholarship fund for which this university had, together with other private schools, lobbied most vigorously, placed it in a position where it could compete with some degree of success with the state university.

Unlike the two schools to be discussed later, the institution's adventure into the Ph.D-granting area has been both selective and erratic. It went further than the first school discussed, but not nearly as far as the next two. It probably would have liked to expand its Ph.D. program more rapidly, but the medical school acted as a brake on such expansion. The combination of the medical school and the expensive Ph.D. program has forced the institution to maintain rather low standards for admission of undergraduates, and the large number of undergraduates, in turn, has forced it to accept many faculty members whose credentials and competencies are less than impressive.

Yet it cannot be said of this school that "he who hesitates is lost"; for given the vast Catholic population in the area where it is located, its fairly vigorous fund-raising drives, and the help from state scholarships, it is in a reasonably sound financial position and probably can survive into the 1970s almost as well as any other private American institution. But it can make little in the way of honest pretensions to any academic quality.

SURVIVAL—BY THE SKIN OF THEIR TEETH The situation of the third Catholic institution can be more accurately specified because a state committee has described it very accurately:

Institution D

Institution D is a private, urban, church-related, coeducational institution. Evening and summer sessions are provided.

Availability of data

The institution provided substantial data regarding student enrollment and faculty assignments; but these data required us to consolidate and convert to a full-time equivalent basis. Information on space assignments, nonacademic personnel, and student employment had to be assembled by the institution for this study, as it was not normally available.

A ten-year forecast which had been prepared in 1965 covering the fiscal years 1963-72 was made available to us. The actual expenditures and income in 1966-67 were substantially higher than those projected into the forecast. Further, our discussions with the institution's administration revealed that its planned development would result in costs substantially above those projected. We, therefore, modified the projection to reflect such costs in order to present a more realistic picture of this study.

Observations and conclusions

Institution D is experiencing rapidly increasing costs of operation which result from the institution's policy of upgrading faculty, staff, and facilities. A major step in the implementation of this policy has been a planning and budgeting approach predicted on program needs rather than budget limitations.

The institution was able to meet these rising costs from current revenue up to 1965-66 mainly through tuition increases and additional gifts and grants. Although additional tuition increases are projected as well as a modest increase in gift and grant income, these resources will be increasingly less than required to maintain a balanced formula operation mainly as a result of its policies on auxiliary activity operations.

(a) Auxiliary Activities While the institution's financial records show a break-even or slight-loss picture on auxiliary activity operations, the cost of such operations did not include a reasonable allocation of administrative, plant operation and maintenance, or dormitory supervision costs. The auxiliary activity space is approximately 40 percent of the total space. Our allocation of indirect costs to the auxiliary activities, therefore, shows what we believe to be a more realistic picture and reveals that this is the main cause of the institution's financial difficulties.

(b) Administration The university lacks a master plan that would correlate program and facilities projects to cost and resource projections. Communication between the academic and financial administrations is not effective.

(c) Faculty Employment There is a stated goal to obtain a higher rating on the AAUP scale for all ranked faculty. The institution's projected costs have been increased to reflect the estimated cost of this objective.

(d) Sources of Income The institution has increased its tuition rates regularly. These increases have not, in the institution's opinion, adversely

affected either the quantity or the quality of the students. Fund-raising efforts have also been increased for the past two years, and both annual and capital gift campaigns have been successful. The projected income from tuition and gifts and grants appears to be attainable.

(e) Treatment of Income Several items of unrestricted income which should have been recorded as current income or as reductions of current expense have been treated as fund changes. For example, in 1965-66 more than $200,000 of such items was assigned directly to funds functioning as endowment. This treatment serves to understate the total unrestricted financial resources which are available to meet operating costs.

(f) Physical Plant The full impact of debt service and maintenance costs on new facilities will not be reflected in expenditures until after 1971. It appears that the institution will have to reassess the projection of its goals and resources before undertaking additional construction.

(g) Statistical and Financial Data

	1963-64	1966-67	1970-71
Credit hours	185,860	199,849	243,672
Faculty-student ratio	1:11.8	1:11.7	1:10.8
Credit hours per faculty member on duty	305	258	282
Average faculty salary			
Professor	$11,387	$14,107	$20,150
Associate professor	9,585	10,916	14,430
Assistant professor	7,942	8,750	11,440
Instructor	6,324	7,170	8,970
Net financial results of current operations by activity (in thousands of dollars)			
Instruction and departmental research	$ 1,434	$ 612	$ 700
Sponsored research	(16)	(105)	(275)
Extension and public service	(56)	(63)	(10)
Auxiliary activities	(606)	(995)	(1,500)
Intercollegiate athletics	(54)	(52)	(30)
Net surplus (deficit)	$ 702	$ (603)	$(1,115)
Cost of instruction per full-time equivalent student	$ 965	$ 1,461	$ 1,854
Cost of instruction per credit hour	$ 37	$ 57	$ 71

In addition to the above information, it may be commented that this school has had an extensive Ph.D. program for many years, a competent faculty, and an intelligent and sophisticated student body. For perhaps a decade it languished under unimaginative administration; then a new administration arrived on the scene and began to vigorously initiate expansion and reforms. Unfortunately, as the state report cited above noted, "communication between the academic and financial administrations is not effective." The financial administration strongly resisted the innovative and expansionist tendencies of the new academic administration, and, at least according to the latter, did not provide adequate information about the financial status of the school. The academic leaders, therefore, apparently were determined to go ahead on their own and ignore the opposition of their financial officers. In the middle of the last academic year, they were informed that initial estimates of income for that year were off by several million dollars. Finally, installing their own financial officer, they discovered to their horror that the school was on the verge of bankruptcy. The situation was temporarily salvaged by liquidating the school's meager endowment, obtaining several large grants, and raising tuition (despite protests from the school's SDS chapter).

The institution's future must be described as cloudy. The academic administrators remain optimistic, though some of the verve and enthusiasm of their initial reform programs have been lost. While the first two schools were examples of conservative financial administrators regulating the schools' expansion, the third school is an example of what happens when communication between imaginative academicians and their financial officers collapses. This particular university, one of the most promising Catholic schools in the country, is in deep trouble because of that collapse in communication. It will probably survive, though barring state aid—state aid, which, it might be noted, involves serious constitutional obstacles—it may have to curtail many of its programs.

MIRACLE SCHOOL In the past 10 years, the fourth institution has constructed $30 million worth of new buildings, has added 350 new secretaries to its payroll, has moved its faculty salaries to the highest of any Catholic university in the country, and has provided offices for its faculty which are better than those to be found in most non-Catholic universities and are the best offices of any Catholic institution in the country. In addition, it is engaged in nationwide recruiting drives which give it students of very high quality and enable it to snatch leading students from top Jesuit high schools all over the country.

These accomplishments are impressive enough, but they are even more impressive when one realizes that the school has always worked with a balanced budget and has never had to go into debt for any of its expansion. Furthermore, it has always been able to turn the Jesuit contributed services back into endowment funds and not use the money to meet operational expenses, although the president of the institution admits that increased operational costs may force the school to dip into the contributed services in years to come. Small wonder, however, that the institution is known as a "miracle school."

Nobody on the campus of the university has any doubts as to who has worked the miracle. The man who has been the president for the last 10 years combines the highest standards of academic excellence with almost unbelievably shrewd financial instincts. The president's instincts for what he could do and what he could not do, in retrospect, seem to have been uncanny. He has combined in his own person the role of both the financial officer and the academic administrator, though at a price of exhausting himself after a decade of service.

We may conclude this brief series of profiles with the observation that Catholic schools can survive and improve as well as any other private institutions if the academic and financial administrations are competent and cooperative. Unfortunately, these conditions are not fulfulled in many, if not most, Catholic schools. While the Catholic schools have no monopoly on either incompetence or bad communications, they are, in all likelihood, more vulnerable to these defects because of their lack of endowment and the uncertainties of the market which they serve.

9. Prospects
for the Future

Whether one sees any rationale for the continuance of Catholic higher education depends to some extent on his view as to what American higher education should look like. If one is convinced that higher education ought to be essentially state-operated on the model of the California or Illinois or New York systems, then there is no rationale for Catholic colleges, or indeed, for any other private schools. If one is willing to concede that it is desirable to have private universities, such as the University of Chicago, and private liberal arts colleges, such as Swarthmore and Reed, then again, one must say that for the foreseeable future there is little rationale for the continuation of Catholic colleges. If, on the other hand, one is persuaded that American higher education is basically sound in its present format, though in need of considerable economic rationalization and the elimination or improvement of inefficient units, then he is not in a position to make a strong case against Catholic or other church-related schools, at least those which are willing to adhere to some kind of standard of quality.

If one is to go even further and to argue that a plurality of "systems" within American higher education is a good thing, and that a variety in higher educational institutions responds to the diverse needs of the different subcultures within the United States and the different personalities of students, he would conclude that there might be much positive merit in the separate Catholic "system," though he would still not know specifically what this merit would be. Manning Pattillo and Donald Mackenzie (1966) in their extensive studies at the Danforth Foundation argue that church institutions "as a whole have substantial assets: freedom to experiment and to serve special purposes; responsiveness to able leadership when provided; close student-faculty relationships; a good record (in some colleges) of preparation for graduate and professional study; concern for the progress of individual students; and espousal of humane values." They go on to say:

Viewed in historical perspective, the church-sponsored institutions belong to the great tradition of collegiate education in the arts and sciences illuminated by the Christian faith. It is a conception of education which, in its essentials, has stood the test of some fifteen centuries. It combines learning in the fundamental fields of knowledge with the insights of the Christian faith, the aim being to cultivate the humane person. Its subject matter changes, but its purposes are fairly constant. At its best it is a broad and general education in that it stresses the arts of thought and communication and the principles which should govern personal and public affairs. It is the most useful kind of education, in the best sense of the word "useful," for its worth is not restricted to a particular occupation, a particular time or place, a particular stratum of society. It should be a liberating, a freeing education. It should provide good preparation for responsible living in a rapidly changing world such as ours. Soundly conceived, it gives the student an understanding of the values that are most worth conserving in our heritage and of how they may be the guiding principles of the future. If there is a single work that describes the highest aspiration of colleges of this type for their graduates, that word is probably "wisdom."

Jencks and Riesman (1967) suggest that secularization and religiousness may coexist on the campus:

Looking to the future, we are constantly tempted to write off the influence of the religious on both academic and non-academic student life, and to assume that all Catholic colleges will eventually serve the same secular professional interests as non-Catholic institutions. But while such a prediction may capture a large part of the truth, it may not be the whole of it. The professions, after all, need not all be secular. The Protestant colleges were secularized because the Protestant clergy lost out in competition with other professional interests, but the Catholic clergy may prove more resilient. The situation in Catholic higher education today, while in some ways similar to that in Protestant higher education a century ago, is by no means identical—if only because the Catholic priests and nuns are better equipped than the Protestant clergy ever was to maintain some sort of distinctive influence over their colleges.

They also see a specific role for Catholic institutions in facilitating modernization within the Church:

In the short run, some Catholic colleges will be able to justify their existency by participating in the renovation of their Church, building morale by attacking the traditionalism which still characterizes so much parish

Catholicism (and a good deal of Vatican Catholicism as well). But creative as these colleges' role may be in the Church, and valuable as they may be in mediating between the conflicting claims of the Church and the academic professions on the young, it is not easy to imagine how this will bring them a continuing supply of talented students. To do that they would have somehow to demonstrate that Catholicism can fertilize the academic disciplines as well as the other way round. Failing that, they are likely to remain predominantly "service institutions," helping move mobile students from the darker to the lighter portions of the occupational and social spectrum but not generating much light themselves.

The two authors are quite correct. Any institutional renovation of Catholicism will not, over the long haul, be a sufficient rationale to maintain the Catholic higher educational "system"; but if we concede to Pattillo and Mackenzie that religious colleges do have a specific contribution to make, particularly in terms of the values of the traditional Christian educational style, we are still forced to specify whether it is possible for there to be a uniquely Catholic style in higher education which is not so much rooted in the ethnic past as it would be in a Catholic vision of the future of man.

The present writer is inclined to believe that there is such a contribution, though he is somewhat skeptical about whether the present leadership in American Catholicism, and Catholic higher education in particular, is creative enough and forceful enough to seek the opportunities inherent in such a Catholic vision of the future.

The Roman Church is presently going through perhaps the greatest upheaval in its history and further carrying off this upheaval with an organizational skill it has not displayed in previous crises for a number of reasons far beyond the concern of this Profile. The elan of Western Catholicism has been weak for the past several centuries, and one is inclined to forget that for a thousand years or more Catholicism preserved the best of the traditions of the past while at the same time pushed eagerly into the future. Much of this tradition has now been secularized and under no conceivable *aggiornamento* process could the Catholic Church ever play the leading cultural role that it played in Western Europe in the Middle Ages. Nonetheless, there are sociological and historical grounds to justify its once again assuming the role of a cultural innovator—an innovator operating out of faith in man's past and hope in man's future. It is certainly not the writer's intention to argue that Catholic higher education ought to be the only innovator or even necessarily the most effective innovator in American higher education. On the other hand, the century-old traditions of Catholicism ought to have equipped Catholic educators with the potential to claim that they are among the wisest of innovators. Such a claim now would be an absurd one, largely because Catholic educators have ignored their own tradition and are content, in many instances, with mere second-rate imitation of what goes on in the rest of American higher education.

It might also be argued that because of its confidence in mankind's future, the Church ought to be a more tough-minded and resilient innovator, willing to take bigger chances in its educational system and much less ready to quit in the face of obstacles and difficulties. It also could be reasonably expected that, given the long concern of Catholic scholars for the integration of knowledge, one would not be unreasonable to suppose that Catholic higher education, if it was to be true to the best of its traditions, would be profoundly concerned about the disorganization of most college curricula. Finally, and to the present author's mind the most important of all, given the concerns now expressed in the catalogs of Catholic colleges of Catholic higher education for the development of the whole man, one would have taken it almost for granted that Catholic colleges and universities would be in the vanguard of those institutions experimenting with the new developmental approach to higher education in which the development of the cognitive elements of the personality takes place in a context of concern for total personality development. The present writer cannot understand why the so-called developmental approach to higher education has not been enthusiastically acclaimed by Catholic educators. Yet men like Nevitt Sanford or Joseph Katz or Kenneth Keniston have never been invited to address meetings of Catholic educators, and one has the vague impression that most Catholic administrators are unaware of their existence or of their stimulating ideas about educational innovation.

The argument of this writer, then, that the major contribution that one can reasonably expect of Catholic higher education in years to come is that it assume the leadership role in experimental innovation in higher education, particularly of the so-called developmental variety.[1] One says that such an expectation is "reasonable,"

---

[1] By "developmental" education we mean, in this context, education which attempts to integrate the intellectual development of the young person with the development of the other facets of his personality. The present writer and his colleagues on the Hazen Committee, in *The Student in Higher Education,* have developed in detail recommendations for innovations along these lines.

not in terms of the past performance of Catholic administrators, but in terms of the traditions and the values of the Catholic Church. Yet at the present time most Catholic schools are so eager to be thought of as being as good as, or at least almost as good as other American institutions, that there is precious little inclination to venture out on their own to attempt educational innovations that are in keeping with their own traditions and before which most of the rest of American higher education hesitates.

One can understand the timidity of the Catholic administrators. For several decades they have been told by both their non-Catholic colleagues and by the self-critics from within that they ought to try to become like other American schools (and sometimes, in the self-critics' terms, this meant like Harvard). Now they are being told that they must be different. There is some contradiction here, but there is also some paradox. The Catholic colleges will never be fully accepted as part of American higher education as long as they try to be as much like Harvard or Reed as they can. They will become accepted only when they respect professional values that are respected at Harvard and Reed and also demonstrate the courage to proceed along the lines of development that are uniquely their own.

One who has doubts about whether Catholic schools are capable of making a unique contribution to American higher education ought merely to visit some of the Catholic colleges which have, for one reason or another, demonstrated the courage to be themselves while at the same time accepting the values of the rest of American higher education. Thus, in all the world, the present writer suspects, there is not a college like Immaculate Heart College in Los Angeles. American higher education would be much richer if there were more IMHC's and much poorer should that gallant institution disappear from the scene. Similarly, St. John's University in Minnesota is conclusive proof that the religious tradition of the Order of St. Benedict can accomplish certain unique things, even in the middle of the twentieth century. Further, some of the better schools run by the religious of the Sacred Heart demonstrate that even the "convent" tradition can be wisely and delightfully modified to train intelligent and lively young women for the twentieth century. Laughter in American higher education is, of course, not limited to Immaculate Heart; links with historical traditions of the past are not limited to St. John's; and community warmth is by no means the monopoly of the religious of the Sacred Heart. Yet these three characteristics receive a special shape at the institutions in question which they would not receive elsewhere. That schools like St. John's, Barat, and Immaculate Heart can adequately fulfill secular standards and still be distinctively Catholic is proof that others can do it too, but it is not a prophecy that they will.

The ideals of American higher education are schools like the University of California at Berkeley, Harvard, Swarthmore, and Reed. Yet one fears that if the higher educational environment was peopled entirely by imitations of these institutions, it would be a dreary place and also quite probably intolerable for the students who would have so little variety to choose from. The University of California at Berkeley is one of the great educational institutions in all the world. San Francisco College for Women (or Lone Mountain, as it is called) is not a university and is not, by most academic standards, even a "great" liberal arts college. And yet this does not mean that the students who attend the latter would receive educations that were "better" for them if they transferred from Lone Mountain to Berkeley. Here, in the judgment of the present writer, is the most important argument for a wide variety in higher educational institutions: There is a wide variety of students; many students will learn more and mature more fully at Berkeley than they would at Lone Mountain. But there are others who will learn more and grow up more healthily at Lone Mountain than they will at Berkeley.

The present writer has no doubt that the Catholic vision of the meaning of man, particularly as it is being reinvigorated in the present transitional crisis in Catholicism, has much to say that would be extremely important to American higher education. Whether there exist the courage and the imagination to put aside the concerns of the immediate past and attempt to implement the Catholic vision of the future in Catholic colleges and universities remains to be seen.

Commentary

Over the last several decades I have visited private and public colleges and universities away from metropolitan centers and have heard faculty members whose own intellectual lives are obviously vivacious complain about the philistinism of their environment, the apathy of their students, and their remoteness from centers of culture and learning. Although the United States is not nearly as centralized as Japan or France, the fear that one is living a provincial life can be almost paralyzing. The people who feel themselves provincial often make two mistakes. They overestimate the sweep of what is happening in more cosmopolitan centers—assuming, for example, that what happens at Harvard or Columbia is exciting, and that students and faculty *there* are brilliant, articulate, dynamic, or whatever; they also tend to underestimate the value of their own situation, for example, that it can be rewarding to work with students who do not start with the narcissistic belief that they are already fully formed or as formed as they need to be, and who regard all requirements as a risk to their independence and self-esteem.

Yet if one comes from an elite institution and says to people at an institution of lesser academic status that there are virtues in their setting, the statement lacks credibility and may sound condescending: a bit like the rich man telling the peasant to be thankful he does not have ulcers—or the white radical telling the lower-class black how wonderful it is not to have intellectual hangups. The real problem here is to find better ways of measuring "value added," that is, what educational institutions do with the students they get (and also with the faculty they recruit). But one cannot measure this in a mechanical way, else one might not give sufficient credit to institutions which already begin with highly precocious people who may therefore be hard to reach, or one might

164

overpraise colleges which move their students a considerable distance but close them off from still further movement. Scarcity of resources, even in a relatively affluent society, means that the question as to who is to be educated, for how long a time, and with what intensity, remains a politically and humanly intricate question, to be resolved neither by defensive provincialism and populist egalitarianism nor by easy meritocratic assumptions as to what the labor force will need in a future that will be partly determined by the decision.

It is impossible to ask people whose position is not privileged, by current social definitions of privilege, to remain in place in order to provide wider cultural and educational diversity. What looks like diversity from outside may be constriction when seen from within. All that the outsider can do is encourage a more variegated sense of potential models of excellence and point out the limitations of models currently being imitated. Andrew Greeley does this in his book in general, and especially in his concluding chapter, although without being very specific as to how an institution may be creatively Catholic after having become aggressively cosmopolitan, other than to say that the trick has indeed been turned at Immaculate Heart College, at Barat, and at St. John's in Collegeville. Whatever inventiveness these institutions possess is the creation principally of the religious in the administration and faculty. Andrew Greeley observes in his book that Christopher Jencks and I, in our chapter on the Catholic colleges in *The Academic Revolution,* raise questions about what appears to be the progressive tendency to substitute lay management as well as lay boards of trustees for administrators and trustees who are members of religious orders. Possibly, this is an inevitable development, not only to appease the anxieties and inferiority feelings of the lay faculty, but because few men and women are now being recruited to the religious life whom one can imagine as potential administrators of an educational institution. Some people of an older generation in the United States as well as in French Canada, entered religious orders or the secular clergy as a form of self-expression in order to accomplish something in a world that would otherwise have constrained them. This was perhaps especially true of young women from backgrounds that were provincial geographically or ethnically. The younger religious, however, seem almost as antiorganizational as the younger radicals among the laity or outside the Church altogether; and like the latter, they often share an antipathy to comfortable, suburban, upper-middle-class whites—preferring, in other words, the inner-city frontier to Manhattanville or Notre Dame. (They resemble in this way many Peace Corps Volunteers I have seen who have compassion for every culture except their own, and who also prefer the poor or the very young to the host culture's bureaucracy and elites.) The last thing these young anarchist radicals with their "Pentecostal" styles of life are willing to do, for example, is to work with college budget officers or to raise money from new-rich Catholics or government officials, and this is so whether their personal style is agressive or amiable, or some combination of both. In an essay on the college presidency, Herbert Simon remarks that money raising is an essential aspect of the allocation of resources among competing academic and non-academic good causes.[1] Andrew Greeley suggests some of the problems that Fordham has faced because its visionary administrators fatefully lacked links to its financial officers—a dichotomy between the academic and the budgetary planners to be found almost everywhere in higher education.

The problem is intensified in all the elite colleges and universities where the responsibility of administrators to maintain the viability of the institution has not been diminished while the legitimacy of authority has been greatly diminished. Some of the Catholic colleges can count on a certain spirit of cohesiveness which has its paternalistic or, as Andrew Greeley rightly notes, maternalistic sides—sometimes more heavy-handed than the actual parents of the young. For faculty trained in leading graduate schools, such institutions may be too familistic. The gossipy net of the religious may seem to close—and feel like a conspiracy.

But in fact there is a lot of ambivalence, both among academics and among students, about the kind of atmosphere they want to find on a campus. Some want an intentional community, repressing ambition and defining it as careerism; repressing leadership and defining it as authoritarianism. In such a setting, the deliquescence of adult authority may only expose people to the pressure of peers each of whom is supposed to do his own thing, which turns out to be almost everyone else's thing—the pressure to be "with it," and to be "relevant" by contemporary shortcuts, can make eccentricity uncomfortable even while avant-garde flamboyance flourishes. *In loco parentis* has such a bad press today that only old fogies among the religious defend it, while deans of women

[1] "The Job of a College President," *The Educational Record,* Winter, 1967, pp. 68-78.

in some state colleges will say a good word at least for hypocrisy vis-à-vis parents and the state legislature. Most parents, when dealing with their own adolescents, find it hard to be authoritative without feeling authoritarian, and many young people thus find no protection from any adults against the tyranny of the peer culture which intrudes upon them in the name of freedom. I believe that colleges need to rethink the issue of *in loco parentis* in order to see if they can do better than the parents as advisers and models, at least in alerting the young to their peer tyrannies and to the pluralistic ignorance of many who dare not confess their fears and naïveté. I doubt if one can do this by formal rules, especially if the rules are not made to show where adults stand but only where they think it politic to appear to stand. But a Catholic college may have available some models of serenity to counter the pressure of evangelists for drugs or nihilism. At a meeting a few years ago of the Catholic Sociological Society, I heard a lay sociologist from a Catholic college talk, with the wry and self-deprecatory style we academics often assume, about the pot and other drug subcultures on his campus, which he felt was very mild and behind the times when compared with Berkeley. I remarked to him afterwards that perhaps his own students were still sufficiently encapsulated so that they would not feel under pressure to show their up-to-dateness by experimenting with drugs; I added that on many campuses the sardonic faculty style he had struck would be a signal to students that they were hopelessly square or behind the times if they had not tried pot or LSD. Since we faculty members have for so long thought of ourselves as a relatively powerless minority, we may not realize how much weight we may carry in our offhand comments.

While it is true that, as Kenneth Keniston, Richard Flacks, Brewster Smith, and other observers of student movements have stated, the "young radicals" generally come from liberal and even radical families, there is a minority of radicals who come from fundamentalist backgrounds. Most Catholics in America, like most Protestant, are not fundamentalist; indeed Catholics have in general accepted the reforms and even the stirring and dispute in the postconciliar Church with a perhaps surprising lack of backlash of the *Wanderer* sort. But one can find, for example, rural German or urban Polish Catholics whose political and cultural as well as religious outlooks are fundamentalist; correspondingly, a few of their college-going children have moved beyond liberalism, cutting themselves off from parents and family with a fierceness that has sometimes made them quasi-leaders in the nonorganizational groupings on the Left, and adopting a new doctrine, a ritual of protest, and a passionate evangelism.

But whereas fundamentalist Protestantism flourishes with the rise in affluence of its adherents, fundamentalist Catholicism is declining, at least among the college-going strata. In an earlier era, the more liberal Catholic colleges sometimes found poor communication as a protection from the Chancery Office or other diocesan controls or from parental vigilantes. Today, still more liberal colleges are not similarly defended from the anxieties of conservative, although not fundamentalist, parents. (There is a general belief that better communication brings enlightenment, but this is often a pious hope). Given the publicity they have had as a result of liberalizing changes, it would be a rare conservative family that would send a daughter to Manhattanville to keep her chaste and simple, or a son to Holy Cross with comparable intent. This is so even though Andrew Greeley's figures show that Catholic graduates of Catholic colleges are more likely to be endogamous and more likely to stay in the fold than the otherwise similar graduates at non-Catholic colleges. This may partly reflect the fact that in the Catholic colleges there is a wider spectrum of faith presented, and partly the more simple fact that the ecological community is more likely to be Catholic. But the style of Catholicism that now prevades many Catholic colleges may be at least as alien to parents as apostasy; better no mass at all than some of the folk masses which may be thought of as black masses by those whose Catholicism was always actually a folk religion.[2]

At any rate, parents who are extremely well-off may make useful rationalizations about why their children would be as likely to remain traditionally devout in the local state college as they would attending a residential Catholic college. I do not think that enrollments will continue to rise in private colleges—in some less-distinguished ones, applications have already taken a turn downward in the face of rising tuition and increasing competition from the state colleges. Certainly the network of urban Jesuit colleges originally established in those many states where the university or the land-grant college was out somewhere "downstate" are faced with increasing competition from places like Wisconsin—Milwaukee, Missouri—St. Louis, Massachusetts—Boston,

---

[2] However, it is wrong to assume that children cannot bring up their parents or bring them along, for example, to a folk mass, which they will enjoy and approve of despite ideological tremors.

Illinois—Chicago Circle, and so on. (The same competition faces the former YMCA colleges like Northeastern and Roosevelt and the urban Methodist colleges like Boston University or the University of Denver.) Certainly, as Andrew Greeley suggests, the Jesuit medical schools are now a financial embarrassment without being much of an academic or scientific asset. Ironically, higher education is an area where it is often the private services which are starved while the public ones are lush and affluent—I have heard students say that they would rather go to the state university with its handsome student center and swimming pool then to the local Catholic college with its undermaintained plant; it takes a state as niggardly toward public higher education as Massachusetts to provide the contrast between Boston College's beautiful faculty offices, to which Andrew Greeley makes reference, and the decrepit, semiconverted office buildings in which the University of Massachusetts—Boston tries to make do.

Yet if the taxpayer backlash against student turbulence (and faculty support for it) continues, all the states may become niggardly—as Congress is now apparently becoming. Private colleges may be better off relatively if the major public universities are forced to cut back on expensive programs which can no longer be funded. If Berkeley and San Francisco State College look less attractive to faculty caught between Right and Left extremes, Lone Mountain or the University of San Francisco or the College of Notre Dame in Belmont may look somewhat more attractive, even when the latter are seeking to shed the vestiges of the monastery or the convent.

Presently both lay and religious faculty members at Catholic colleges are eager to sponsor their able students on to graduate schools—usually, as Andrew Greeley has observed, outside the Catholic orbit. Indeed, the fact that Catholics from Catholic colleges are more likely to go on in academic life may in part reflect the eager sponsorship of faculty, which is more than Catholics would get in other colleges without such concern for nurturing talented students.[3] As Joseph Zelan has shown in work growing out of studies done at NORC, the academic career itself becomes a kind of

[3] Everett Hughes has called my attention to the need to compare Catholics taking similar courses or programs in Catholic and non-Catholic colleges before one could jump to such a conclusion. Undeniably the faculty in Catholic colleges are eager to encourage academic "vocations," but as Andrew Greeley notes, Catholics in non-Catholic colleges are apt to be in practical fields like commerce, engineering, or pre-law in contrast to the probably somewhat wealthier undergraduates attending the liberal arts programs of Catholic institutions.

religion for its devotees, and they want converts among the young to sustain their own faith as well as to open opportunities which they regard as rewarding.[4] For those Catholic colleges that do not go into the Ph.D. business in order to hold faculty, sending students on to the major graduate schools is the next best thing.[5]

Andrew Greeley speaks of the inferiority complex haunting Catholic higher education especially among the avant-garde whom James Trent terms the "critical devout." Yet criticism of one's own institution—not to speak of ethnic group or nation—is characteristic of the American avant-garde generally. And the better the institution, the freer the criticism. The relative degree of pluralism within American Catholicism is presently so enormous that one could substitute the word "American" for "Catholic" at many points in Andrew Greeley's analysis and take account in that case also of the existence of several traditions, absolutist and pluralist, on which different groups may draw. The belief that Catholicism is monolithic, like the belief that America is, reflects a desire to simplify reality so that one is never disappointed or surprised. Yet one of the many negative consequences of this form of mild paranoia is that it minimizes the interest of social phenomena and cramps curiosity.

Andrew Greeley is well aware that curiosity concerning the idiosyncratic details of all the sects that make up American Catholicism tends to get lost from view and requires a historian like Philip Gleason to rediscover them. There is indeed a Catholic tradition which is systematic and nonempirical, reflected in some of the conflicts within the theology departments, not only on the more traditionalist side but also in such freewheeling theologians as write for *Continuum* or *Cross-Currents.* The relative weakness of the more concrete social sciences in the Catholic colleges is therefore particularly sad, although it should be added that the social sciences everywhere suffer in varying degrees from overgeneralization (to be sure, other wings of social science suffer from a monotonous empiricism that is no great improvement over grandiosity). This is one reason why a work of social science like the volume

[4] Joseph Zelan, "Religious Apostasy, Higher Education and Occupational Choice," *Sociology of Education,* vol. 41, no. 4, pp. 370-379, Fall, 1968.

[5] A companion volume in this series, Alden Dunham's *Colleges of the Forgotten Americans* (McGraw-Hill, 1969), makes clear that many newly arrived state universities are so enamored of graduate programs as to pay less attention to their undergraduates; to the extent that these latter are Catholic, they may be less likely to receive the kind of personal support that the Catholic liberal arts colleges, like some of the small Protestant ones, do provide.

in hand is important for Catholics no less than for non-Catholics. Whether the kind of developmental education that Andrew Greeley recommends at the close of his volume would serve such concrete learning is, for me, not clear. Much depends on what is really meant by the "whole person" on whose development many Catholic colleges pride themselves. Will this in the current climate feed the sort of passionate emotionalism that regards factuality as a constraint and sees research as a delaying tactic in the war against racism, poverty, and other social evils? Some educators along with many students have come to prefer grandiose amateurs to competent specialists. They may have picked up Thorstein Veblen's term, "trained incapacity," to hurl at the technocrat while Veblen used the term to refer to the gentleman of leisure and not to his admired engineers. A focus on the whole person may be liberating when advocated in such a West Point of science as Rice University and stultifying in a setting where it may serve to justify a comfortable incompetence where no one is ever stretched to the limit of his powers.

Catholic colleges, like other colleges, ought to be aware that the doctrine of "wholeness" is an abstraction or a metaphor like any other and that the lacunae in a student's development may be quite idiosyncratic to him at that time and that place.[6]

I remember visiting Notre Dame nearly two decades ago, and sharing with some of the lay and religious faculty a shudder at the tiresome "Catholic" Gothic architecture and the small place given to aesthetic sensibility. Today, Notre Dame's achievements in science and engineering need to be protected against the spokesmen of a sentimental humanism all the more compelling because it feels itself defeated. It would also be a loss if the insistent rationality that has been associated with the best Jesuit education in the past were dropped in favor of sensitivity training. I would hope (and so, I think, would Andrew Greeley) that Catholic colleges would remain different from each other even if they face some of the common problems of all higher education: the common problems of coping on the one side with docile or passive students from the lower middle class who are barely enlightened and with students from the upper middle class who reject any education that is not a happening.

Members of religious orders do have one often unsuspected asset

[6] For some proposals along this line, see my essay "The Search for Alternative Models in Education," *The American Scholar,* vol. 38, no. 3, pp. 377 - 388, Summer, 1969.

in reacting to the latter category of students which arises from the discipline, in several senses of the term, that religious who are also academicians must undergo and try to maintain. The formation of a priest and even of a nun has in the past produced college teachers who are often limited in their intellectual range.[7] Today, however, the ambiguities that face the budding seminarian can seldom be resolved either by the clichés of an earlier more doctrinaire Catholicism or by those that circulate in the youth culture as a substitute for thought and for individualization. Just as I have come to feel that a medically trained therapist is likely, because of the rigor of medical training, to be a safer bet as a therapist than a clinical psychologist, even though the latter may have had slightly less irrelevant training, so the demands of the religious vocation operate not, of course, always to select morally, let alone intellectually, superior men and women, but at least to sift out some of those who are obviously self-indulgent and unserious. To the degree that liberal arts colleges in the Catholic orbit can retain some religious on their faculties, they may add to the range of models with which young men and women are confronted, and, hence, complicate these models. This may be especially important for those who in earlier parochial schooling were too immature to recognize the idiosyncratic qualities of the nuns in the classroom and, hence, to get a sense of the dilemmas of all vocations, including those they might themselves choose.

David Riesman

[7] For critical accounts of both lay and religious academic styles see John D. Donovan, *The Academic Man in the Catholic College* (Sheed & Ward Inc., 1964); also John D. Donovan, "The American Catholic Hierarchy: A Social Profile," *The American Catholic Sociological Review*, XIX, pp. 98-113, 1958.

References

Ahern, P. H.: *The Catholic University of America, 1887-1896,* Catholic University of America Press, Washington, D.C., 1948.

Barry, C. J.: *Worship and Work: Saint John's Abbey and University, 1856-1956,* St. John's Abbey, Collegeville, Minnesota, 1956.

Davis, James A.: *Great Aspirations,* Aldine Publishing Company, Chicago, 1964.

Ellis, J. T.: "American Catholics and the Intellectual Life," *Thought,* 30 (Autumn), 351-388, 1955.

Gleason, P.: in R. Hassenger (ed.), *The Shape of Catholic Higher Education,* John Wiley, New York, 1967.

Greeley, A. M.: *Religion and Career: A Study of College Graduates,* Sheed and Ward, New York, 1963.

Greeley, A. M.: "Influence of the 'Religious Factor' on Career Plans," *The American Journal of Sociology,* LXVIII (No. 6, May), 658-671, 1963.

Greeley, A. M.: "Religion and Academic Career Plans," *The American Journal of Sociology,* LXXII (No. 6, May), 668-672, 1967.

Greeley, A. M.: *The Changing Catholic College,* Aldine Publishing Company, Chicago, 1967, 8-9; 128-130; 177-180; 190-191; 193-194.

Greeley, A. M., and P. H. Rossi: *The Education of Catholic Americans,* Aldine Publishing Company, Chicago, 1966.

Hamilton, R. N.: *The Story of Marquette University,* Marquette University Press, Milwaukee, 1953.

Jencks, C., and D. Riesman: "The Catholics and Their Colleges (I)," *The Public Interest,* (No. 7, Spring), 90-93; 94, 1967.

Jencks, C., and D. Riesman: "The Academic Revolution," *The Public Interest,* (No. 8, Summer), 55-58, 1967.

Knapp, R. H., and H. B. Goodrich: *Origins of American Scientists,* University of Chicago Press, Chicago, 1952.

Knapp, R. H., and J. J. Greenbaum: *The Young American Scholar: His Collegiate Origins,* University of Chicago Press, Chicago, 1953.

Lenski, Gerhard: *The Religious Factor,* Doubleday and Company, New York, 1960.

O'Dea, Thomas: *American Catholic Dilemma,* Sheed and Ward, New York, 1958.

Patillo, Manning M., Jr., and Donald Mackenzie: "Conclusions and Recommendations," in *Church-Sponsored Higher Education in the United States,* Report of the Danforth Commission, American Council on Education, Washington, D.C., 1966, 198.

Power, E. J.: *A History of Catholic Higher Education in the United States,* Bruce, Milwaukee, 1958.

Trent, James: *Catholics in College,* University of Chicago Press, Chicago, 1967.

Warkov, S., and A. M. Greeley: "Parochial School Origins and Educational Achievement," in *American Sociological Review,* 31, 1966, 406-414.

Appendix: Catholic Institutions of Higher Education in the United States

These 388 institutions are tabulated from those designated as under Catholic control in the National Center for Educational Statistics, U.S. Department of Health, Education, and Welfare, Opening Fall Enrollment in Higher Education 1966, *U.S. Government Printing Office (Washington, D.C., 1967).* Groupings are according to listings in the Department of Education, United States Catholic Conference and Secretariat of the National Conference of Catholic Bishops, The 1967 Official Guide to Catholic Educational Institutions, *Catholic Institutional Directory Co. (New York, 1967).* Some Catholic institutions are not, for one reason or another, listed in the U.S. Office of Education materials. Other published compilations include closely related institutions under a single entry.

COLLEGES AND UNIVERSITIES FOR LAYMEN

Alabama
St. Bernard College
Spring Hill College

California
College of the Holy Names
College of Notre Dame
Dominican College of San Rafael
Immaculate Heart College
Loyola University of Los Angeles
Marymount College
Mount St. Mary's College
St. Mary's College of California
San Francisco College for Women
University of San Diego College for Men
University of San Diego College for Women
University of San Francisco
University of Santa Clara

Colorado
Loretto Heights College
Regis College

Connecticut
Albertus Magnus College
Annhurst College
Fairfield University
Sacred Heart University
St. Joseph College

District of Columbia
Catholic University of America
Dunbarton College of the Holy Cross
Georgetown University
Trinity College

Florida
Barry College
Biscayne College Incorporated
St. Leo College

Hawaii
Chaminade College of Honolulu

Illinois
Barat College of the Sacred Heart

College of Saint Francis
De Paul University
Lewis College
Loyola University
Mundelein College
Quincy College
Rosary College
St. Dominic College
St. Procopius College
St. Xavier College

Indiana
Marian College of Indianapolis
St. Benedict College
St. Francis College
St. Joseph—Main Campus
St. Mary of the Woods College
St. Mary's College
University of Notre Dame

Iowa
Briar Cliff College
Clarke College
Loras College
Marycrest College
Mount Mercy College
St. Ambrose College

Kansas
Marymount College
Mount St. Scholastica College
Sacred Heart College
St. Benedict's College
St. Mary's College
St. Mary of the Plains College

Kentucky
Bellarmine College
Brescia College
Catherine Spalding College
Nazareth College of Kentucky
Ursuline College
Villa Madonna College

Louisiana
Loyola University
St. Mary's Dominican College
Xavier University

Maine
St. Francis College
St. Joseph's College

Maryland
College of Notre Dame of Maryland
Loyola College
Mount St. Agnes College
Mount St. Mary's College
St. Joseph College

Massachusetts
Anna Maria College for Women
Assumption College
Boston College
Cardinal Cushing College
College of the Holy Cross
College of Our Lady of the Elms
Emmanuel College
Merrimack College
Newton College of the Sacred Heart
Regis College
Stonehill College

Michigan
Aquinas College
Madonna College
Marygrove College
Mercy College of Detroit
Nazareth College
St. Mary's College
Siene Heights College
University of Detroit

Minnesota
College of St. Benedict
College of St. Catherine
College of St. Scholastica
College of St. Teresa
College of St. Thomas
St. John's University
St. Mary's College

Missouri
Avila College
Fontbonne College
Maryville College of the Sacred Heart

Rockhurst College
St. Louis University
Webster College

Montana
Carroll College
College of Great Falls

Nebraska
Creighton University
College of St. Mary
Duchesne College of the Sacred Heart

New Hampshire
Mount St. Mary College
Notre Dame College
Rivier College
St. Anselm's College

New Jersey
Caldwell College for Women
College of Saint Elizabeth
Georgian Court College
St. Peter's College
Seton Hall University

New Mexico
College of Santa Fe
University of Albuquerque

New York
Canisius College
College of Mount St. Vincent
College of New Rochelle
College of St. Rose
Dominican College of Blauvelt
D'Youville College
Fordham University
Good Counsel College
Iona College—Main Campus
Ladycliff College
LeMoyne College
Manhattan College
Manhattanville College of the Sacred Heart
Marist College
Mater Dei College
Marymount College
Marymount Manhattan College

Mercy College
Molloy Catholic College for Women
Mount St. Mary College
Nazareth College of Rochester
Niagara University
Notre Dame College of Staten Island
Rosary Hill College
St. Bernardine Siena College
St. Bonaventure University
St. John Fisher College Incorporated
St. John's University
St. Francis College
St. Joseph's College for Women
St. Thomas Aquinas College

North Carolina
Belmont Abbey College
Sacred Heart College

North Dakota
Mary College

Ohio
College of Mount St. Joseph on the Ohio
College of St. Mary of the Springs
College of Steubenville
Mary Manse College
Notre Dame College
Our Lady of Cincinnati College
St. John College of Cleveland
University of Dayton
Ursuline College for Women
Walsh College
Xavier University
John Carroll University

Oregon
Maryhurst College
Mount Angel College
University of Portland

Pennsylvania
Alvernia College
Cabrini College
Chestnut Hill College
College Misericordia
Duquesne University

Gannon College
Gwynedd-Mercy College
Holy Family College
Immaculata College
King's College
LaRoche College
LaSalle College
Marywood College
Mercyhurst College
Mount Mercy College
Rosemont College
St. Francis College
St. Joseph's College
St. Vincent College
Seton Hill College
University of Scranton
Villa Maria College
Villanova University

Rhode Island
Providence College
Salve Regina College

South Dakota
Mount Marty College

Tennessee
Christian Brothers College
Siena College

Texas
Incarnate Word College
Our Lady of the Lake College
Sacred Heart Dominican College
St. Edward's University

St. Mary's University
University of Dallas
University of St. Thomas

Vermont
College of St. Joseph the Provider
St. Michael's College
Trinity College

Washington
Fort Wright College of the Holy Names
Gonzaga University
St. Martin's College
Seattle University

West Virginia
Wheeling College

Wisconsin
Alverno College
Cardinal Stritch College
Dominican College
Edgewood College of the Sacred Heart
Holy Family College
Marian College of Fond du Lac
Marquette University
Mount Mary College
Mount Senario College
Mount St. Paul College
St. Norbert College
Viterbo College

Puerto Rico
Catholic University of Puerto Rico
College of the Sacred Heart

JUNIOR COLLEGES FOR LAYMEN

Alabama
Sacred Heart College

District of Columbia
Immaculata College

Florida
Marymount College

Illinois
St. Bede Junior College
Springfield Junior College

Indiana
Ancilla Domini College

Iowa
Mount St. Clare College
Ottumwa Heights College

Kansas
Donnelly College

Kentucky
St. Catherine College

Maryland
Mount Providence College
Villa Julie College Incorporated

Michigan
DeLima College

Minnesota
St. Mary's Junior College

Missouri
Mercy Junior College
St. Mary's Junior College

New Jersey
Edgewood Cliffs College

Immaculate Conception Junior College
Tombrock College

New York
Elizabeth Seton College
Immaculata College
Maria College of Albany
Maria Regina College
Queen of the Apostles College
Sancta Maria College
Villa Maria College of Buffalo

North Dakota
Assumption College

Oklahoma
St. Gregory's College

Pennsylvania
Mount Aloysius Junior College

South Dakota
Presentation College

Texas
Christopher College of Corpus Christi

Virginia
Marymount College

COLLEGES FOR RELIGIOUS

California
College of Our Lady of Mercy
St. Joseph College of Orange

Connecticut
College of Notre Dame of Wilton
Diocesan Sisters College
St. Basil's College
Seat of Wisdom College

Illinois
Delourdes College

Louisiana
Our Lady of the Holy Cross College

Maryland
St. Mary's Seminary and University
Xaverian College

Massachusetts
College of the Sacred Hearts
Mount Alvernia College

Michigan
Maryglade College

Missouri
Marillac College
Notre Dame College

New York
Brentwood College

Mary Rogers College
Mount St. Joseph College

Rhode Island
Catholic Teachers College
Mount St. Joseph College

JUNIOR COLLEGES FOR RELIGIOUS

Connecticut
Mount Sacred College

Florida
St. Joseph College of Florida

Illinois
Felician College
Immaculata College
Mallinckrodt College

Kentucky
Loretto Junior College

Maryland
Thivenet Institute

Minnesota
Corbett College

New Jersey
Assumption College

New York
Catherine McAuley College
College of the Holy Names
St. Clare College

Ohio
Lourdes Junior College

Pennsylvania
Sacred Heart Junior College

SEMINARIES

California
St. Albert's College
St. John's College
St. Patrick's College
San Luis Rey College

Colorado
St. Thomas Seminary

Connecticut
Holy Apostles Seminary
Holy Family Seminary
St. Alphonsus College

St. Mary's Seminary
St. Thomas Seminary

District of Columbia
Holy Cross College
Oblate College
St. Joseph's Seminary
St. Paul's College

Idaho
College of St. Gertrude

Illinois
Aquinas Institute of Philosophy and Theology

Divine Word Seminary
Maryknoll Seminary
St. Mary of the Lake Seminary
Tolentine College

Indiana
Crosier House of Studies
St. Meinrad Seminary

Iowa
Divine Word College

Kentucky
St. Thomas Seminary

Louisiana
Notre Dame Seminary
St. Joseph Seminary

Maine
Oblate College and Seminary

Maryland
St. Peter's College
Trinitarian College
Woodstock College

Massachusetts
Aquinas School
Marist College and Seminary
Queen Apostles College and Seminary
St. Columban's College and Seminary
St. Hyacinth College and Seminary
St. John's Seminary
St. Stephen's College

Michigan
Duns Scotus College
Sacred Heart Novitiate
Sacred Heart Seminary
St. John's Provincial Seminary

Minnesota
Crosier Seminary
St. Paul Seminary

Mississippi
Our Lady of the Snows Scholastica

Missouri
Cardinal Glennon College
Immaculate Conception Seminary
Kendrick Seminary
St. Mary's Seminary

New Hampshire
Queen of Peace Mission Seminary
St. Anthony's Seminary

New Jersey
Don Bosco College
Immaculate Conception Seminary
St. Michael's Passionist Monastery
St. Joseph's College

New York
Buffalo Diocesan Preparatory Seminary
Catholic College of the Immaculate
   Conception
Epiphany Apostolic College
Hillside Hall Junior College
Immaculate Conception Seminary
La Salette Seminary
Maryknoll Seminary
Mater Christi Seminary
Mount St. Alphonsus Seminary
Our Lady of Hope Mission Seminary
Passionist Monastic Seminary
St. Bernard's Seminary and College
St. John Vianny Seminary
St. Joseph Seminary Catholic College
St. Joseph Seminary College—Main Campus
St. Joseph's Seraphic Seminary
St. Pius X Preparatory Seminary
St. Pius X Seminary
Wadhams Hall Seminary

Ohio
Athenaeum of Ohio
Borromeo Seminary of Ohio
Pontifical College Josephium
St. Mary's Seminary

Oregon
Mount Angel Seminary

Pennsylvania
Blessed Sacrament College

Kilrose Seminary of the Sacred Heart
Mary Immaculate Seminary
St. Charles Borromeo Seminary
St. Fidelis College and Seminary

Rhode Island
Seminary of Our Lady of Providence

Texas
Oblate College of the Southwest

Virginia
Father Judge Mission Seminary

Washington
Sulpician Seminary of the Northwest

Wisconsin
DeSales Preparatory Seminary Incorporated
Immaculate Conception College
St. Francis College
St. Francis Seminary
St. Lawrence Seminary

Index